access to history

HENRY VII

Second Edition

Roger Turvey
and Caroline Rogers

D0274384

Hodder & Stoughton

A MEMBER OF THE HODDER HEADLINE GROUP

Acknowledgements

The front cover shows Henry VII by an anonymous artist, reproduced courtesy of the National Portrait Gallery, London.

The publishers would like to thank the following individuals, institutions and companies for permission to reproduce copyright illustrations in this book:

Cardiff City Council, page 16; The Board of Trustees of the Victoria & Albert Museum, page 21; Public Record Office Image Library, page 72; The Bridgeman Art Library, page 120; The Trustees of the British Museum, page 121.

The publishers would also like to thank the following for permission to reproduce material in this book:
Extracts from *The Wars of the Roses*, C Carpenter, Cambridge University Press, 1997; Extract from 'Henry VII and the English Nobility' by TB Hugh in *The Tudor Nobility*, GB Bernard (ed), Manchester University Press, Manchester, 1992; Shepheard-Walwyn Publishers Ltd for CRN Routh, *Who's Who in Tudor England*, London, 1990; Extract from *Henry Tudor and Wales*, Glanmor Williams, University of Wales Press, Cardiff, 1985.

Every effort has been made to trace and acknowledge ownership of copyright. The publishers will be glad to make suitable arrangements with any copyright holders whom it has not been possible to contact.

Orders: please contact Bookpoint Ltd, 78 Milton Park, Abingdon, Oxon OX14 4TD. Telephone: (44) 01235 827720, Fax: (44) 01235 400454. Lines are open from 9.00–6.00, Monday to Saturday, with a 24-hour message answering service. Email address: orders@bookpoint.co.uk

British Library Cataloguing in Publication Data
A catalogue record for this title is available from The British Library

ISBN 0 340 75381 1

First published 1991, 2000
Impression number   10 9 8 7 6 5 4 3 2
Year   2005 2004 2003 2002 2001

Copyright © 2000 Roger Turvey and Caroline Rogers

Typeset by Fakenham Photosetting Ltd, Fakenham, Norfolk.
Printed in Great Britain for Hodder & Stoughton Educational, a division of Hodder Headline Plc, 338 Euston Road, London NW1 3BH.

Contents

Preface

To the general reader

Although the *Access to History* series has been designed with the needs of students studying the subject at higher examination levels very much in mind, it also has a great deal to offer the general reader. The main body of the text (i.e. ignoring the 'Study Guides' at the ends of chapters) forms a readable and yet stimulating survey of a coherent topic as studied by historians. However, each author's aim has not merely been to provide a clear explanation of what happened in the past (to interest and inform): it has also been assumed that most readers wish to be stimulated into thinking further about the topic and to form opinions of their own about the significance of the events that are described and discussed (to be challenged). Thus, although no prior knowledge of the topic is expected on the reader's part, she or he is treated as an intelligent and thinking person throughout. The author tends to share ideas and possibilities with the reader, rather than passing on numbers of so-called 'historical truths'.

To the student reader

Although advantage has been taken of the publication of a second edition to ensure the results of recent research are reflected in the text, the main alteration from the first edition is the inclusion of new features, and the modification of existing ones, aimed at assisting you in your study of the topic at AS level, A level and Higher. Two features are designed to assist you during your first reading of a chapter. The *Points to Consider* section following each chapter title is intended to focus your attention on the main theme(s) of the chapter, and the issues box following most section headings alerts you to the question or questions to be dealt with in the section. The *Working on . . .* section at the end of each chapter suggests ways of gaining maximum benefit from the chapter.

There are many ways in which the series can be used by students studying History at a higher level. It will, therefore, be worthwhile thinking about your own study strategy before you start your work on this book. Obviously, your strategy will vary depending on the aim you have in mind, and the time for study that is available to you.

If, for example, you want to acquire a general overview of the topic in the shortest possible time, the following approach will probably be the most effective:

1. Read chapter 1. As you do so, keep in mind the issues raised in the *Points to Consider* section.
2. Read the *Points to Consider* section at the beginning of chapter 2 and decide whether it is necessary for you to read this chapter.
3. If it is, read the chapter, stopping at each heading or sub-heading to note down the main points that have been made. Often, the best way of doing this is to answer the question(s) posed in the *Key Issues* boxes.
4. Repeat stage 2 (and stage 3 where appropriate) for all the other chapters.

If, however, your aim is to gain a thorough grasp of the topic, taking however much time is necessary to do so, you may benefit from carrying out the same procedure with each chapter, as follows:

1. Try to read the chapter in one sitting. As you do this, bear in mind any advice given in the *Points to Consider* section.
2. Study the flow diagram at the end of the chapter, ensuring that you understand the general 'shape' of what you have just read.
3. Read the *Working on ...* section and decide what further work you need to do on the chapter. In particularly important sections of the book, this is likely to involve reading the chapter a second time and stopping at each heading and sub-heading to think about (and probably to write a summary of) what you have just read.
4. Attempt the *Source-based questions* section. It will sometimes be sufficient to think through your answers, but additional understanding will often be gained by forcing yourself to write them down.

When you have finished the main chapters of the book, study the 'Further Reading' section and decide what additional reading (if any) you will do on the topic.

This book has been designed to help make your studies both enjoyable and successful. If you can think of ways in which this could have been done more effectively, please contact us. In the meantime, we hope that you will gain greatly from your study of History.

Keith Randell

1 Introduction

POINTS TO CONSIDER

The aim of this chapter is to give you a brief background of later medieval England so that you will understand and remember the main concepts and issues of the period before proceeding to a detailed study of the reign of Henry VII.

1 Historical Background

KEY ISSUE What is faction and how did it contribute to causing the dynastic struggle known as the Wars of the Roses?

> 1 We will unite the white rose and the red:
> Smile, heaven, upon this fair conjunction
> That long hath frowned upon their enmity! ...
> Now civil wounds are stopped, peace lives again:
> 5 That she may long live here, God say Amen!

These were the words that William Shakespeare, writing about a century after the events he was describing, chose to place into the mouth of Henry VII at the moment he became king. They reflect the typical late-sixteenth-century Englishman's view of the nature of the achievements of the founder of his country's current dynasty; Henry Tudor was seen as the monarch who brought the turmoil of the recent civil war to an end, uniting the rival houses of Lancaster and York. This book will investigate the accuracy and completeness of the judgement.

On 22 August 1485 Henry Tudor, Earl of Richmond, defeated Richard III at the Battle of Bosworth and was subsequently crowned Henry VII of England. His reign lasted 24 years. When he died from natural causes in 1509, his son was immediately proclaimed king and was crowned two months later. It is a tribute to the success of his government that Henry VII was the first English monarch for nearly 100 years to pass on his crown undisputed to his son. His character remains shadowy and elusive but his achievements were very real. Although he has been eclipsed in the history books by Henry VIII and Elizabeth I, his reign made possible their success.

Bosworth was the final act in the civil conflict known as the Wars of the Roses which had dominated England's political, social and economic life throughout the fifteenth century. For this reason 1485 is often seen as a watershed in the history of England. It is a date frequently used as a division between what historians call the medieval and the early modern periods. The reign of Henry VII ended the civil war and heralded the foundation of a new dynasty, the Tudors, under whom England was transformed. It is convenient to divide history up in this way, but it must be remembered that this is only done to make the past easier to understand. Although periods of history tend to be studied in isolation, it is necessary to understand the context within which each is set if the large degree of continuity there was from 'period' to 'period' is to be appreciated. It will be helpful, therefore, to consider briefly the events that were Henry VII's legacy when he ascended the English throne in 1485.

The Wars of the Roses were a dynastic struggle between two families (and their supporters) who believed that the crown of England rightfully belonged to them. The Plantagenets had ruled England more or less unchallenged until 1399, when some members of the upper classes became disillusioned with the weak, arbitrary and authoritarian rule of Richard II. His cousin, Henry Bolingbroke, Duke of Hereford (1397) and Earl of Derby (1377), who had a distant claim to the throne, mustered enough support to win the crown for himself. Henry IV, as he became, was the son of John of Gaunt, Duke of Lancaster, himself a younger son of Edward III (see family tree page 3). Stability eventually returned to England under the rule of Henry and a measure of his success was the undisputed accession of his eldest son, Henry V, in 1413. Englishmen lamented Henry V's premature death in 1422, not only because he had won for them the great victory of Agincourt against the French and had united the two countries by his marriage to a French princess, but also because it left as their king a minor, the baby Henry VI. Ironically, England emerged from the period of minority rule relatively unscathed and it was only when the adult Henry assumed the reins of government himself that serious problems arose again. This was partly due to his bouts of mental instability but was also because his academic and saintly personality was not suited to the demands of medieval kingship. Henry was easily manipulated by his ambitious nobles who banded together to form factions, each vying to control the king. Confidence in Henry was further shaken with the loss of all the French lands so recently won by his father. Law and order finally disintegrated as, in desperation, men took up arms against the king and his favourites. In this unsettled climate another claimant to the throne – Richard, Duke of York (see family tree) – put himself forward. Throughout the 1450s the two families of Lancaster and York fought for the crown. In the past, the destruction caused by this struggle has been exaggerated by historians. In reality, most of the battles were nothing more than skirmishes affecting only a small percentage of the population. As we shall see later, their real effect was on the structure of society.

In 1461 the Yorkist claimant, Edward, Duke of York (the son of Richard, Duke of York), was able both to defeat Henry VI and to take control of London, where he was crowned king as Edward IV.

Lancastrians, Yorkists and Tudors

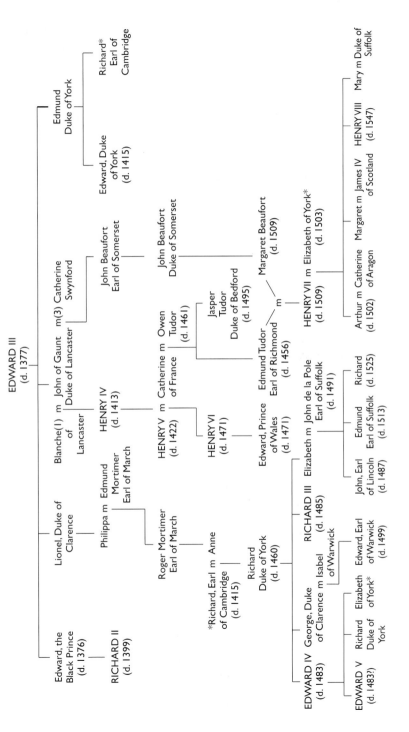

Once again England had a strong leader, and he strove to attain peace at home and prestige abroad. Unfortunately, he died unexpectedly in 1483, leaving his 12-year-old son as heir. The succession was thrown into turmoil again when Edward's brother, Richard, seized the throne for himself. Historians have long been perplexed about why Richard acted in this aggressive way, having been so loyal to Edward throughout his reign. The most widely held view is that he acted on the spur of the moment to prevent the queen's family from robbing him of the position of regent. There has also been a great deal of speculation about the fate of the two young sons of Edward, 'the Princes in the Tower', neither of whom was seen alive again. However, all was not to run smoothly for Richard. He lost much support in the aftermath of his usurpation, and court and country became disunited again. It was in this atmosphere that the distant Lancastrian claimant, Henry Tudor, decided that the time was ripe for him to try his hand at winning the crown of England.

2 The Geography of Henry's New Kingdom

> **KEY ISSUE** What was the territorial extent of Henry VII's kingship and power?

The geographical extent of Henry VII's inheritance consisted of England as we know it today, stretching from Cornwall in the south-west to the northern border marked by Hadrian's Wall. It also included Wales and Ireland, but these were ruled in a somewhat different manner to the rest of the country because of the way in which they had come to the crown. Wales consisted of the Principality (made up of what later became the counties of Anglesey, Caernarfon, Merioneth, Denbigh, Flint, Cardigan and Carmarthen), the Marcher Lordships (made up of the lands on either side of the modern boundary between England and Wales), and, in the south, the Crown Earldoms of Glamorgan and Pembroke. These had their own systems of government, different from each other and from that of England. Both the Principality and the Lordships owed allegiance to the king of England and he had ultimate control over them, but the absence of continuous effective rule from London had resulted in frequent outbreaks of disorder. Geographically more distant and far more of a problem was Ireland, where the king was referred to as 'Lord'. The only part of the island in which the king's orders were obeyed was the small area round Dublin known as the Pale. The rest of Ireland was divided into Anglo-Irish earldoms (ruled over by the descendants of Englishmen who had landed to make their fortunes earlier in the Middle Ages), and Gaelic clans, whose chieftains were native Irish. No king had been able to dominate these lords and so Ireland remained very much a law unto itself. It posed a potentially explosive problem

Map of England, Scotland, Ireland, Wales and coast of France

to any king of England, but particularly to a new and inexperienced one. Scotland was officially independent of England and had its own king, but the fact that he owed allegiance to the king of England had led to a tradition of bitter hostility between the two countries. Another serious problem with Scotland was the country's strategic position as the back door into England, particularly for France, the traditional enemy. This was a familiar element in England's foreign policy and was a factor that Henry would have to take into account. English kings continued to style themselves king of France despite the fact that since the reign of Henry VI the only French territory they still possessed was Calais. This rankled with the French and did nothing to foster good relations between the two countries.

3 Society and Economy

> **KEY ISSUE** What were the key features of English society and the nation's economy?

In the late fifteenth century England was primarily a rural society and about 95 per cent of the population lived off the land. Scattered amongst the numerous villages that together made up the English landscape were about 700 towns, all small except London which numbered around 50,000 people, about two per cent of the total population of the country. The other larger provincial towns together made up another two per cent, but even the most important of these, such as Norwich or Bristol, did not exceed 10,000 people, and most had under 1,000.

At the end of the fifteenth century the population of England was about 2,250,000. It was during Henry's reign that numbers began to increase steadily for the first time since the fatal outbreak of plague, the Black Death of 1348–9, which had killed about a third of the population of western Europe. The population increase continued until the middle of the seventeenth century and is of major importance in studying this period. It meant that there were fewer jobs than there were people to fill them and there were more mouths to feed. One bad harvest would mean real hunger for many, and could lead to widespread unrest.

Another feature of English society in the later middle ages was the breakdown of the feudal system. William the Conqueror had developed this after the Norman Conquest as a way of controlling his new kingdom. It was based on the relationship between lord and vassal: the vassal rendered services in return for land held from the lord. One of these feudal services was fighting for one's lord when required. This provided the monarch with a relatively efficient armed force when he needed it. As time went on dues were paid for in cash or in goods rather than in personal service, and this trend was hastened by the decline in the population after the Black Death. The peasants found that their labour was in high demand and exploited it. The feudal system began to collapse as peasants moved around to find the highest wages or found land that could be rented cheaply with no feudal obligations attached.

4 The Government of late Medieval England

> **KEY ISSUE** What were the main problems facing government in fifteenth-century England?

The government of medieval England was in the hands of the king and whoever he chose to advise him and to sit on his council. It was an age of personal monarchy when the king ruled in the fullest sense of the word and this meant the country prospered or stagnated depending on the ability of each ruler. In 1471 Sir John Fortescue, Chief Justice of the King's Bench under Henry VI, wrote *The Governance of England* which offered Edward IV advice on how to restore political strength and stability. Fortescue identified the financial weakness of the crown as the major problem and he advocated retrenchment (cutting down on expenditure) and re-endowment (re-investment, or finding other ways of raising money for the crown) to halt this decline. Another weakness was the increasing power of the nobility. During the Wars of the Roses nobles had seized their opportunity to take control of the provinces, so that it was their orders that were obeyed rather than those of the king. If Henry was to prove himself a strong king and establish full control of his realm he would have to subdue these over-mighty subjects and reverse this trend.

By far the largest landowner in the country, besides the king, was the Church. In 1485 this was the Roman Catholic Church and its first allegiance was not to the English crown but to the pope in Rome. It formed a state within a state, with its own system of law courts and privileges available for the clergy, which superseded the authority of the king. Although this was potentially an explosive situation, crown and Church normally managed to exist side by side in relative harmony. Henry VII was a good son of the Church and did nothing to jeopardise this: that would be left to his son, Henry VIII, in the following reign.

5 Cultural Developments

> **KEY ISSUE** To what extent had the continental Renaissance and the printing press impacted on English culture and society?

The dramatic cultural developments which were taking place on the continent in a movement which we call the Renaissance (the 'rebirth' of art, architecture and letters) came late to England. Mainly it took a literary form known as humanism, rather than the artistic form which was more typical in Italy. Humanism was the return to the study of the original classical texts and to the teaching of the humanities as the basis of civilised life. It made its first appearance in England in the middle of the fifteenth century. Because literacy was confined to the upper echelons of society, its devotees were restricted to the educated upper class. The most famous humanist scholar, Erasmus, visited England for the first time in 1499 and was impressed with the high standards of classical teaching being fostered by John Colet, Dean of St Paul's Cathedral and founder of St Paul's School. However, this was an isolated development and an extended humanist circle did not emerge until the reign of Henry VIII.

Perhaps the most significant event of this period was the arrival of the printing press, brought to England in 1476 by William Caxton from Germany. Edward IV was happy to act as patron, and from this point a steady stream of major English texts and translations from French and Latin emerged from the press. This led to the growth of a wider reading public, the beginnings of the standardisation of the English language and the circulation of the radical ideas of Erasmus and, after 1517, Martin Luther. Henry VII also made use of it to spread propaganda justifying his succession to the throne and denouncing the rule of Richard III. Throughout this book you will find various extracts from a history of England written by Polydore Vergil and commissioned by the king.

The majority of Englishmen were devout followers of the traditional practices and beliefs of the Church. Their main preoccupations were death and judgement, heaven and hell. The religious fervour of the laity was frequently expressed in a materialistic way, and in the fifteenth century many of England's parish churches were either built or were improved by individuals hoping that their generosity would help reserve a place for them in heaven. The only heretical ideas to have acquired a significant following in England in the later middle ages were those of Lollardy. This laid stress on the reading of the Bible and urged the clergy to confine themselves to their pastoral duties. However, systematic persecution in the early fifteenth century had forced it underground, and there was no resurgence under Henry VII.

6 History's Treatment of Henry VII

KEY ISSUE How far has history's treatment of Henry VII changed?

The views of historians on the achievements of Henry VII have varied over the centuries. The judgements of earlier historians were influenced by the traditional assessment of the fifteenth century which was hampered by inadequate knowledge and coloured by a traditional view of this time as superstitious and uncivilised. For example, Edward Hall published his Chronicle in 1547 and entitled it 'The union of the two noble and illustrious families of Lancaster and York, being long in continual dissension for the crown of this noble realm'. He saw Henry as the saviour of England after the civil strife that had dogged the country since Henry IV's usurpation in 1399. Shakespeare continued this theme in his history plays, making Henry VII's main aim 'to unite the white rose and the red'. One of the most influential assessments of Henry's reign until this century was *The Life of Henry VII* by Francis Bacon, first published in 1622. His praise for Henry was probably intended to gain the favour of Henry's descendant, James I, as the picture he paints of Henry is similar to how James saw himself. It is from him that such memorable phrases as 'a wonder for wise men', and 'this Solomon of England' spring. Bacon saw Henry as master of his own realm and 'arbiter in Europe'. This eulogy misled later historians and led them to exaggerate Henry's achievements. By the late nineteenth century the 'New Monarchy' theory had arisen. This was the belief that Henry, having rescued England from the ravages of civil war, proceeded dynamically to restructure the government of the country. He was cast as an innovator in the art of government. Today, with more extensive research available on the later middle ages, Henry's methods of government seem far less revolutionary and, in fact, very similar to those of his immediate Yorkist predecessors. The most outstanding work written this century is the study of Henry's reign by S.B. Chrimes. He argues that Henry was an essentially medieval monarch but that he gave England the stability it needed after the Wars of the Roses. Henry's methods of government may be seen as medieval, but it is necessary for every student of early Tudor history to understand why he resorted to well-tried methods and then to assess how consistent and successful he was in implementing them.

Summary diagram

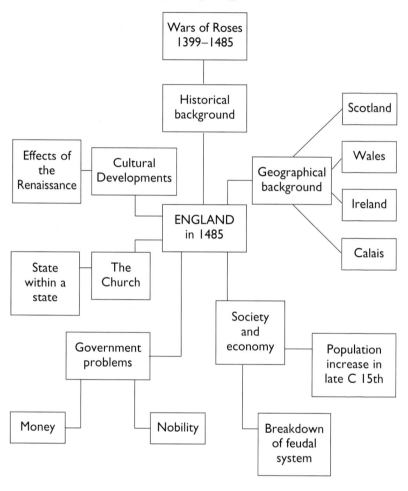

Working on Chapter 1

This chapter aims to provide you with useful background information which, if you have no prior knowledge of the period, should serve you well as a starting point. If you are near the beginning of your course you should make a point of writing down the meaning of any terms that you have not met before. This is a good habit which should be repeated for every chapter you read.

You may wish to make brief notes on the different sections within this chapter either by answering the questions in the issues boxes or, alternatively, by using the summary diagram as a framework for what you write. Each box could be used as a heading. If you wish to confine your note-making to the most important sections within the chapter then you should concentrate on 'Historical Background' and 'History's Treatment of Henry VII'.

You are unlikely to be asked to write in detail about Henry VII and England before 1485 but you may wish to broaden your understanding of the period. If so, then you must be selective in your choice of reading, which should be limited to general histories such as those listed at the back of this book in the section headed Further Reading. On the other hand, you may wish to use technology to save valuable time. The most efficient way in which you could do this is by using the internet. Unless you know a particular address you should use a search engine by typing in key words such as 'Wars of the Roses', 'the Tudors' or 'Henry VII'. The internet will prove to be a useful tool which you should resort to periodically as you work through this book.

2 Establishing the Tudor Dynasty

POINTS TO CONSIDER

This chapter considers the reason why Henry Tudor claimed the crown of England and how he secured the throne after winning the Battle of Bosworth. It then considers the different challenges the king faced to his crown and how he dealt with them. Your aim should be to concentrate on the pretenders to Henry's throne and the rebellions. You should ensure that you are clear about who was behind them, and why, and how successfully Henry suppressed them.

KEY DATES

1457 Birth in Pembroke Castle, Wales, of Henry, son of Edmund Tudor, Earl of Richmond and Margaret Beaufort.

1471 Yorkist victories at the battles of Barnet and Tewkesbury forced Henry and his uncle Jasper into exile in Brittany.

1485 Battle of Bosworth in which Henry secured the throne by defeating and killing King Richard III. Henry crowned as King Henry VII.

1486 Marriage of Henry and Elizabeth of York.

1487 Battle of Stoke in which Henry defeated disaffected Yorkists and their pretended leader Lambert Simnel. Birth of a son, Arthur, to Henry and the crowning as queen of his wife, Elizabeth.

1489 Rebellion in Yorkshire over taxation put down.

1495 Landing, in Deal, Kent, and failure of attempted rebellion by Perkin Warbeck.

1497 Rebellion in Cornwall over taxation eventually suppressed after the rebels reach Blackheath on the outskirts of London. Warbeck taken prisoner after abortive rising in West Country.

1499 Warbeck and the Yorkist Earl of Warwick executed.

1 Henry's Claim to the Throne

> **KEY ISSUES** What was the basis of Henry VII's claim to the throne? What impact did his early life and exile have on the future king?

To the majority of Englishmen the Battle of Bosworth on 22 August 1485 was just one more skirmish in the long struggle for the crown that dominated the second half of the fifteenth century. On this occasion the victor happened to be the obscure Lancastrian claimant, Henry of Richmond. The 28-year-old earl was an unknown entity to his new subjects, most of whom would have believed his chances of remaining on the throne to be extremely slim. It was only victory in battle that had brought Henry to power, as his claim to the throne by inheritance was rather weak. It lay through his mother, Margaret Beaufort, who was a direct descendant of Edward III by the marriage of his third son, John of Gaunt, Duke of Lancaster, to Katherine Swynford (see the family tree on page 3). Their children had been born when Katherine was Gaunt's mistress and, although an act of parliament in Richard II's reign had legitimised them, a further act in Henry IV's time had excluded them from the throne. Henry VII also inherited royal blood, although not a claim to the throne, from his father Edmund Tudor, whose mother, Catherine, was a French princess who had been married to Henry V of England before she became the wife of Edmund's Welsh father, Owen Tudor.

a) Early Life

If we are to attempt to understand Henry's actions as king and to discover the character of the man behind the mask of kingship, it is vital to take into account the unusual circumstances of his early life. His childhood was unsettled and coloured by the civil war from the very beginning. He was born in Pembroke Castle on 28 January 1457, the only child of Edmund Tudor, Earl of Richmond and Margaret Beaufort. His mother was only 14 years old and his father had died of some epidemic disease three months earlier.

Henry of Richmond spent his early years at Pembroke Castle with his mother, but in 1461 after the defeat of the Lancastrian king, Henry VI, the castle was seized by Sir William, later Lord, Herbert. While Henry VI and his son were still alive, the young earl was no more to the new Yorkist king, Edward IV, than a valuable ward. This meant that because Henry's father was dead, and he was a minor, Edward, as his feudal lord, would control both him and his estates. In 1462 Edward sold the guardianship of Henry to Lord Herbert for £1,000, and transferred the overlordship of the Richmond lands to his own brother, the Duke of Gloucester. From this point Henry saw little or nothing of his mother. She was married again in 1464 to Henry Stafford, second son of the Duke of Buckingham and, after his death in 1471, to Lord Thomas Stanley. According to the chronicler Polydore Vergil, who later wrote a history of England, Henry was 'kept as prisoner, but honourably brought up' in the Welsh-speaking Herbert household at Raglan Castle in south-east Wales and educated as a prospective son-in-law. Circumstances changed in 1469 when, defeated in battle, Herbert was executed by the Earl of Warwick, and Henry VI was briefly restored in 1470. When this temporary Lancastrian interlude terminated with the deaths of Henry VI and his only child, Prince Edward, the following year, Henry, Earl of Richmond, suddenly became the main Lancastrian claimant to the throne. Jasper Tudor, Earl of Pembroke, recognising the vulnerable position into which fate had flung his nephew, took him across the Channel to safety.

b) Years in Exile

Henry remained in exile for 14 years, mostly in Brittany – then an independent duchy in what is now modern-day France – as the guest of its ruler Duke Francis II. Polydore Vergil records that Edward IV reacted 'very grievously' to the news that 'the only imp now left of Henry VI's brood' had escaped and he offered a substantial reward for the return of the two fugitives. However, the duke stood by his guests, although he did promise to guard them so that they would not escape and harm Edward IV. Perhaps he also realised how useful they might be in future negotiations with England and France. At any rate, their English servants were sent home and replaced by Bretons and Edward IV had to be satisfied with that. Later, in 1475, after he had made a favourable treaty with Louis XI of France, Edward renewed his attempt to bring Henry back to England by persuading Duke Francis that he wanted to marry Henry to one of his daughters. The duke was in a difficult position because had he refused there was a risk of England and France uniting and endangering Brittany's independence. However, Henry himself resolved the situation. Convinced that he would be going to his death if he were handed over to the English Embassy at St Malo, he fell into a fever, or pretended to, which delayed his crossing. One of the duke's favourite advisers persuaded Francis that Henry's fate was indeed precarious and, while the English ambassadors were conveniently distracted, Henry was rescued and taken into sanctuary. Duke Francis renewed his promise to guard Henry, and Edward IV made no further attempt to retrieve him. Throughout this period Jasper Tudor and Henry remained in contact with Lancastrians at home, although there is no evidence that they ever challenged Edward's claim to be king.

In 1483 the situation changed when Richard, Duke of Gloucester, proclaimed himself king on the sudden death of his brother, Edward IV. Edward's two young sons disappeared in suspicious circumstances and Richard's former ally, the Duke of Buckingham, turned against him. Once again the political climate in England became unsettled. By usurping the throne and denying the succession of his nephew, Edward V, Richard had laid himself open to challenge. Henry Tudor therefore changed from being an obscure claimant to a secure Yorkist throne to being a potential rival to Richard III. Those dissatisfied with Richard's actions began to plot to replace him with Henry Tudor. Margaret Beaufort and Edward IV's widow, Elizabeth Woodville, were drawn into the conspiracy. They agreed that Henry should marry Edward's daughter, Elizabeth, which should help him to attract both Lancastrian and Yorkist support. However, Buckingham ruined the plan by a precipitous rising which led to his execution in November 1483. Meanwhile, Henry had set sail in mid-October, but his fleet was dispersed by a storm and he sensibly refused to land at Plymouth without the certain knowledge of support. Safely back in Brittany, he determined to maintain the loyalty of his new followers, some of whom were former Yorkists. Consequently, at a public ceremony in Rennes Cathedral on Christmas Day 1483, he solemnly swore that if he were to win the throne that was rightfully his from Richard III, he would make Elizabeth of York, the major Yorkist heiress, his queen. Henry hoped that this pledge would not only consolidate the support he already had, but would also win others over to his side, as this would be the first step towards a union of the two rival families which had fought for the crown for the last 30 years.

Henry's return to Brittany was soon threatened by Richard III's intervention in Breton politics. Richard took advantage of the illness of the elderly Duke Francis to put pressure on the councillors who were acting in his place to surrender Henry Tudor. Fortunately, Henry was warned in time by an English refugee, John Morton, Bishop of Ely. In a swiftly conceived plan, Henry escaped to France disguised as a servant. When Duke Francis recovered, he was furious about what had happened and arranged for the remainder of the English party, numbering about 300, to be conducted safely to Henry.

Henry slowly began to gather an English court around him in Paris as the nobility became increasingly discontented with the actions of Richard III. After the deaths of Richard's son and heir and his queen, rumours began to spread that he intended to make his niece, Elizabeth of York, his bride, thus thwarting Henry's plan. Polydore Vergil tells us that in these circumstances Henry was 'ravished with joy' to greet the Earl of Oxford, a loyal Lancastrian, to his side. Other future Tudor councillors also joined him: Edward Poynings from England, Bishop Morton from Flanders, Richard Fox, who abandoned his studies in Paris, and lesser men who had been involved in the abortive rising in 1483. Thus Henry was able to plan a new invasion; the Earl of Oxford and Jasper Tudor providing the necessary military expertise, while his other adherents were a source of vital information about the conditions and sympathies of different parts of England.

JASPER TUDOR

Born c. 1431 at Hatfield, Hertfordshire. Created Earl of Pembroke in 1452 by his half-brother Henry VI.

Ruled South Wales on behalf of King Henry VI from 1457 to 1461.

Fled into exile after defeat in the battle of Mortimer's Cross in 1461.

Armed expedition to North Wales ended in failure. Deprived of his earldom and title.

Restored to power during Henry VI's brief second reign, 1470–71.

Fled for a third time into exile after the Lancastrian defeat at the battle of Tewkesbury, 1471. He took his nephew, Henry, with him.

Spent the next fourteen years (1471–85) bringing up his nephew and

Victorian stained glass picture of Jasper Tudor in Cardiff Castle.

protecting him from various Yorkist plots intended to murder him. Celebrated victory in the battle of Bosworth (1485).

Restored to his Earldom of Pembroke and created Duke of Bedford (1485). Married the widow of the Duke of Buckingham.

After ten years' loyal service, Jasper Tudor died in 1495.

1 One of the great survivors of the age, Jasper, almost alone among the major participants, came through the civil wars of 1455 to 1485 unscathed. During those tempestuous years, he proved himself to be the most loyal and tenacious upholder of the Lancastrian cause, on behalf of
5 first Henry VI and his son, and later, of his nephew Henry. For thirty years, in face of adversity, defeat and long years of penurious exile in Scotland, Brittany and France, as well as setbacks in England, he never once yielded, as far as we can tell, to the temptations of despair, treachery, or changing sides.

Sir Glanmor Williams, *Henry Tudor and Wales* (Cardiff, 1985)

1 For all stromes it wolle endure,
It is trusty atte nede,
Now the sayle-yearde I wolle rehearse,
5 The Erle of Pembroke, curtys and ferce,
Across the mast he lyethe travers,
The good ship for to lede.

He is the hope of our language;
Great is the grace that Jasper was born of the blessed stock of Cadwaladr ...

Jasper has been ordained for us, to pull us free from the net about us ...

Two contemporary poems, composed by an Englishman and Welshman respectively, heap praise on Jasper Tudor.

2 The Battle of Bosworth: Henry becomes King

> **KEY ISSUES** How did Henry achieve victory at Bosworth? What kind of man was Henry VII?

a) The Road to Bosworth

It is important to remember that Henry could never have contemplated invading England without financial assistance from abroad. Charles VIII of France was willing to provide this in the hope that it would distract Richard III from sending help to Brittany and allow the French to annex the duchy quickly. Henry set sail from Harfleur on 1 August 1485, accompanied by between 400 and 500 loyal exiles who had joined him, and at least 1,500 French soldiers, although the latter were not of the best quality. The expedition sailed for Wales hoping for a good reception in Henry's homeland. He landed at Mill Bay near Dale in Pembrokeshire on 7 August and marched northwards along the Cardiganshire coast, turning inland through the Cambrian mountains and along the river Severn to the border with England. By 12 August Henry had won over Rhys ap Thomas, the most influential landowner in South Wales, with the lure of the Lieutenancy of Wales should Richard be defeated. He reached Shrewsbury on 15 August with an army swollen to around 5,000 men, mainly Welsh recruits, but could not hope to win a battle unless he obtained more support from the English nobility. Henry's main hope lay with two brothers – his stepfather, Lord Stanley, and Sir William Stanley – whose lands included much of North Wales, Cheshire and the Borders. They sent money, but did so secretly as Richard held Lord Stanley's eldest son a prisoner as hostage for his father's good behaviour. However, Henry was confident enough of their support to march further into England, gaining the additional support of Gilbert Talbot, the powerful uncle of the Earl of Shrewsbury and 500 of his men.

Richard was in residence at Nottingham Castle when he learnt of the invasion. He did not act immediately because he thought that his rival would be defeated in Wales by either Rhys ap Thomas in the south, or the Stanleys in the north. When he realised his mistake, he moved his troops to Leicester. The two armies confronted each other just outside the small village of Market Bosworth in Leicestershire on 22 August. Henry's forces now numbered about 6,000, Richard's forces outnumbering them two to one. The records do not make clear whether or not this included the Stanleys' force of 3,000, which remained on the sidelines for most of the battle. No eyewitness account of the battle exists but, by piecing together later accounts, we learn that fighting began early in the morning with Henry's forces charging across a marshy area towards the king's army. The battle only lasted about three hours, but was bitterly contested with heavy casualties on both sides. The turning point came when Richard impetuously decided to strike at Henry himself. He almost succeeded, slaughtering Henry's standard bearer before his personal guard closed ranks. At this crucial moment Henry's step-uncle, Sir William Stanley, waiting in the wings to see the direction in which the battle would go, rushed to his rescue. Richard's death concluded the battle and the leaderless Yorkists fled. Lord Stanley himself picked up the crown from 'the spoils of battle' – not the legendary hawthorn bush – and placed it on Henry Tudor's head. Richard's naked body was tossed over a mule and taken to Leicester to be buried. The long years in exile were over for Henry.

b) Character of the new King

The personality of Henry VII remains shadowy and elusive today, just as it was to his own subjects in 1485. There is less evidence about him than about any other of the Tudors. He emerges from history books as a rather enigmatic character, in stark contrast to the vivid and ebullient personalities of his son, Henry VIII, and his granddaughter, Elizabeth I, about whom contemporaries wrote at great length. However, the uncertainty about the personality of the first Tudor monarch is typical of many of his medieval predecessors. For example, the controversy surrounding Richard III shows how limited evidence can lead to widely differing opinions. Accounts written in his lifetime tell us that he was rather shy, slightly built and may have had a crooked shoulder. Influenced by Tudor historians after his death, people began to think of him as an evil-looking hunchback. Today people are still divided over why he seized the throne from his nephew, Edward, and whether he murdered the princes in the Tower. Similarly, historians tend to disagree about Henry's character, mainly because kings rarely recorded their own thoughts, with the result that historians have had to draw their own conclusions from Henry's actions and policies. However, some of the views of his contemporaries still exist. Among the more interesting, if not necessarily the most useful, is the portrait of Henry VII (on the front cover) by Sittow, a talented artist of the northern Renaissance in Flanders. It was painted from an actual sitting in 1505.

The following description is by Polydore Vergil, a brilliant Italian scholar who arrived at the English court in 1501. Henry was so impressed by his understanding of history that he urged him to write a history of England. This is Vergil's description of Henry in his *Anglica Historia*:

1 His body was slender, but well built and strong; his height above the average. His appearance was remarkably attractive and his face was cheerful, especially when speaking; his eyes were small and blue, his teeth few, poor and blackish; his hair was thin and white; his complexion sallow. His
5 spirit was distinguished, wise and prudent; his mind was brave and res-

olute, and never, even at moments of the greatest danger, deserted him. He had a most pertinacious memory. With all he was not devoid of scholarship. In government, he was shrewd and prudent, so that no-one dared to get the better of him through deceit or guile. He was gracious and kind

10 and was as attentive to his visitors as he was easy of access. His hospitality was splendidly generous; he was fond of having foreigners at his court ... but those of his subjects who ... were generous only with promises he treated with harsh severity ... He was most fortunate in war, although he was more ... inclined to peace ... He cherished justice

15 above all things... He was the most ardent supporter of our faith ... and daily participated with great piety in religious services ... but all these virtues were obscured latterly by avarice ... In a monarch indeed it may be considered the worst vice, since it is harmful to everyone.

It is useful to compare Vergil's description with the impression that we gain from studying Sittow's portrait. Vergil is probably more candid because he wrote a few years after Henry's death, and was therefore not concerned about provoking the king's displeasure.

At Henry's funeral John Fisher, Bishop of Rochester, gave the oration:

1 His politic wisdom in governance was singular ... his reason pithy and substantial, his memory fresh and holding, his experience notable, his counsels fortunate and taken by wise deliberation, his speech gracious in diverse languages ... his dealing in time of perils and dangers was cold

5 and sober with great hardiness. If any treason was conspired against him it came out most wonderfully.

Francis Bacon's *History of the Reign of King Henry VII*, published in 1622, remained the major work on the reign until this century. He describes Henry as 'one of the best sort of wonders: a wonder for wise men', but 'for his pleasures, there is no news of them'. This implies that Henry was admired for his intellectual ability but that his lifestyle was rather colourless. Bacon intended his *History* to be more than a factual account of the past 100 years, and wanted his contemporaries and future generations to learn from it. Therefore he passed judgement on those who came under his scrutiny. He writes that Henry:

1 Professed always to love and seek peace ... For his arms, either in foreign or civil wars, were never unfortunate ... He was of a high mind, and loved his own way; as one that revered himself, and would reign indeed. Had he been a private man he would have been

5 termed proud: but in a wise prince, it was but keeping of distance, which indeed he did towards all; not admitting any near or full approach neither to his power or to his secrets. For he was governed by none.

The avaricious monarch in the famous nursery rhyme, sitting permanently in his counting house counting out his money, was based on Henry VII. Because he devoted so much of his time to replenishing the crown's empty coffers, historians have accused him of being a miser. You will be able to assess how far you judge this to be an accurate conclusion when you have read Chapter 4. In fact, his account books make fascinating reading, for we catch a glimpse of Henry the man, as well as Henry the king. From them we discover his weakness for dicing and playing cards, and the way he indulged his own and his younger daughter's love of music, spending 13s 4d on 'a lute for my lady Mary' and £2 'to the princess's string minstrels at Westminster'. This 'miserly' king was rash enough on occasions to pay £30 'for a little maiden that danceth' and to spend £13 6s 8d on a leopard for the Tower menagerie! A European visitor commented on his sumptuous table, 'I had the opportunity of witnessing twice' for 600 guests. He was a keen sportsman, playing tennis and chess regularly, but his great passion was the hunt and he kept an impressive stable of horses. Henry is remembered as rather a cold man but the warmer, more human side was revealed on the death of his eldest son, Prince Arthur, when he rushed to comfort his wife, and when Elizabeth herself died 'he privily departed to a solitary place and would no man should resort unto him'. In order to gain a satisfactory picture of Henry's complex personality you have to read the available source material, which is limited, and then, having studied his policies, come to a fuller conclusion of your own (see the source-based questions at the end of this chapter).

3 How Henry Secured the Throne

> **KEY ISSUE** By what means did Henry secure the throne?

Henry Tudor was King of England through blood and conquest. He was the male heir of the House of Lancaster through his mother, whose own claims as heiress were ignored, partly on account of her gender, but mainly because in such turbulent times the warring factions needed an adult male capable of leading them into battle. However, it was the victory at Bosworth which secured Henry's claim to the throne. Henry's first actions revealed his concern about the succession and his desire to stress the legitimacy of his position, regardless of defeating Richard or his marriage to Elizabeth of York. For example, he dated the official beginning of his reign from the day before Bosworth. Therefore Richard and his supporters could be declared traitors. This was doubly convenient because it meant that their estates became the property of the crown by act of attainder – attainders were acts of parliament registering a person's conviction for treason and declaring all his property forfeit to the king. Henry

Henry VII by Pietro Torrigiano *c*.1508–9

deliberately arranged his coronation for 30 October, before the first meeting of parliament on 7 November. Thus, although this body granted the riches of the crown to Henry and his heirs, it could never be said that parliament made Henry VII king. Soon after Bosworth, Henry applied for a papal dispensation to marry Elizabeth of York. This was necessary because they were distant cousins. The necessary document did not arrive until 16 January 1486. Henry and Elizabeth were married two days later, finally uniting the Houses of Lancaster and York. The inevitable delay in obtaining the dispensation conveniently ensured that no-one could say that Henry owed his crown to his wife.

After Bosworth, Henry's most immediate and perhaps greatest problem was ensuring that he kept the crown. Although many potential candidates had been eliminated from the succession during the Wars of the Roses and their aftermath, it was not until 1506 that Henry could feel really secure on his throne. By that time the most dangerous claimants to the crown were either dead or were safely behind bars.

In 1485 there were still a number of important Yorkists alive with a strong claim to the throne. The most direct male representative of the family was Richard III's 10-year-old nephew, the Earl of Warwick. Henry successfully neutralised him temporarily by sending him to the Tower. Although it was a royal stronghold, the Tower was also a royal residence, so Warwick lived in relative comfort although without the freedom to come and go as he pleased. Richard had named another nephew, John de la Pole, the Earl of Lincoln, as his heir. However, both he and his father, the Duke of Suffolk, professed their loyalty to Henry and the king accepted this. Lincoln was even invited to join the council. Although Richard's supporters at Bosworth were naturally treated with suspicion, Henry was prepared to give them a second chance as long as he could be persuaded of their loyalty to him. The Earl of Surrey had fought on the Yorkist side with his father, the Duke of Norfolk who died at Bosworth, and Henry kept him in prison until 1489 when he became convinced of his good intentions. However, another of Richard's allies, the Earl of Northumberland, was released even sooner, at the end of 1485, and was given the opportunity to prove his loyalty by resuming his old position in control of the north of England. Henry also attempted to ensure the obedience and support of two other leading Yorkist northern Lords. He demanded financial sureties from Viscount Beaumont for his good behaviour, and kept the heir of the Earl of Westmorland at court. Ex-Yorkists were therefore not automatically alienated from the Tudor court: loyalty was the new king's only requirement for them to regain royal favour.

4 Minor Risings, 1485–6

> **KEY ISSUES** Who was responsible for the risings of 1485–6? How were the risings suppressed?

In spite of his precautions, Henry faced a minor rising before the first anniversary of his accession. Although, with hindsight, it appears rather insignificant, it was alarming for Henry at the time as he could not tell how much Yorkist sympathy might be aroused by it. Trouble broke out while the king was on royal progress to his northern capital of York. This was a public relations exercise in an unruly area, whereby the king showed himself to his people in an attempt to secure their support. Since Bosworth, Francis, Lord Lovel, one of Richard's most loyal supporters, and the Stafford brothers, Thomas and Humphrey, also faithful adherents of Richard, had been in sanctuary at Colchester. The Church offered protection from the law for up to 40 days but, by the fifteenth century, sanctuaries in major towns were sheltering people for indefinite periods of time, although this was a source of dispute with some kings. As Henry travelled north in April 1486, the three lords broke sanctuary. Lovel headed north and planned to waylay the king, while the Staffords travelled to Worcester to stir up rebellion in the west. Henry heard of this while he was at Lincoln but, in order to show his confidence, he continued with his progress. He dealt with the situation by sending an armed force to offer the rebels the choice of pardon and reconciliation or, if they fought and lost, excommunication and death. The rebels dispersed, but Lovel evaded capture once more and fled to Flanders. The Staffords sought sanctuary once again. The king and his judges felt that it was unreasonable for declared traitors to be allowed sanctuary a second time, so the Staffords were arrested and sent to the Tower. Humphrey was executed but Thomas was pardoned and remained loyal thereafter.

Here Henry's calculated mercy was apparent. His policy of severity towards the major ring-leaders and clemency to the rank and file proved successful. The royal progress to the disaffected areas provoked the required reaction of loyalty and obedience, and Henry was seen as the upholder of justice and order. As if to put the seal on this success, the queen gave birth to a healthy son on 19 September at Winchester, England's ancient capital. Evoking memories of the country's great past, the baby was christened Arthur. The king was not yet 30 years old – young enough to sire more children and to see his heir attain maturity.

5 Lambert Simnel, 1486-7

> **KEY ISSUE** How serious a challenge to Henry's rule was Lambert Simnel's rebellion?

Henry was king because he had defeated Richard III in battle. The nature of the usurpation meant that a rising from Richard's Yorkist followers, such as Lovel and the Staffords, was almost inevitable. However, if such a plot was to have more chance of success in the future then the conspirators needed a Yorkist replacement around whom they could weave their plans. In the absence of an available Yorkist descendant, suitable candidates were found who could impersonate one of the Yorkist princes in the Tower. The careers of the two pretenders, Lambert Simnel and Perkin Warbeck, were of great significance to Henry VII. They presented such a dangerous challenge to his hold on the crown both because of their entanglement with other European states, particularly Burgundy, and because they lingered on for such a long time.

a) Origins of Simnel's Rebellion

Oxford and its environs were traditionally Yorkist. So it is not surprising that the first of the pretenders originated from there. Throughout the winter of 1486 conflicting rumours circulated about the fate of the Earl of Warwick. Many concluded that he must be dead, as he had not been seen for some time. In this unsettled climate, a 28-year-old priest from Oxford, Richard Symonds, seized his opportunity. He detected a striking resemblance between one of his pupils, the 10-year-old Lambert Simnel, the son of an organ maker, and the murdered sons of Edward IV. Symonds decided to pass Simnel off as the younger boy, Richard of York. However, in the light of fresh rumours about the Earl of Warwick, he seems to have changed his mind and to have decided that Simnel would now impersonate Warwick. Symonds took his protégé to Ireland, a centre of Yorkist support ever since Richard, Duke of York (the father of Edward IV and Richard III), had been Lord Lieutenant there in the 1450s. The present Lord Lieutenant, the Earl of Kildare, and other Irish leaders, readily proclaimed Simnel as Edward VI in Dublin. The pretender was also supported by Edward IV's sister, Margaret, Dowager Duchess of Burgundy, who was always ready to seize an opportunity to strike at Henry. She sent a force of 2,000 German soldiers to Ireland, commanded by the capable Martin Schwarz. This formidable support led the Irish to go as far as to crown Simnel as King Edward VI in Dublin in May 1487, although they had to improvise the crown, borrowing a coronet from a nearby statue of the Virgin Mary!

Although the conspiracy must have begun in the autumn of 1486, Henry himself does not appear to have been aware of it until New Year 1487. In February 1487 a few lesser nobles were declared traitors and Edward IV's queen, Elizabeth Woodville, and her son by her former marriage, the Marquess of Dorset, were put under house arrest and deprived of their lands. What exactly they were thought to have done remains obscure. The real Earl of Warwick was exhibited in London to expose the imposter. But the problem was not so easily resolved. The sudden flight of the Earl of Lincoln to join the elusive Lord Lovel in Flanders at the court of his aunt, Margaret of Burgundy, made clear the gravity of the situation. Lincoln then accompanied Lovel and Schwarz to Ireland in May 1487. It is probable that the earl had been involved from an early stage. Lincoln obviously knew that Simnel was an impostor, but possibly planned to put forward his own claim to the throne when he judged the time to be right.

b) The Suppression of the Rebellion: The Battle of Stoke, 1487

Henry showed his concern by offering a pardon to such long-standing rebels as Thomas Broughton. He was fearful, not knowing how many of his leading subjects would defect to the Yorkist cause when the crisis came to a head. On 4 June 1487 Lincoln and his army landed at Furness in Lancashire, marched across the Pennines and then turned south. He received less support than he expected because people were weary of civil strife and the reputed wild behaviour of the Irish soldiers probably dissuaded some from joining the rebels. The king, expecting an invasion via Ireland, was prepared and the two armies met in Nottinghamshire, at East Stoke, just outside Newark, on 16 June 1487. Lincoln's forces numbered about 8,000 and Henry's possibly totalled 12,000, but many held back even on the battlefield itself. The immediate attack of the experienced German soldiers and the daredevil tactics of the Irish severely strained the royal front line, but after three hours it was the Yorkist forces that were divided and surrounded. Lincoln, Schwarz, Broughton, and Thomas Geraldine, the Irish leader, all perished, along with nearly half their army. Lovel either disappeared or was killed: certainly he was never seen again. Lambert Simnel and Richard Symonds were both captured. Symonds was sentenced to life imprisonment in a bishop's prison out of respect for his clerical position. The king, recognising that Simnel had been merely a pawn in the hands of ambitious men, made him a turnspit in the royal kitchen. He was later promoted to be the king's falconer as a reward for his good service! Henry's calculated mercy was apparent yet again. He could afford to be reasonably generous to Simnel because Symonds was now in prison and the real ringleaders were dead. As a deterrent to others in the future, those nobles who had fought at Stoke were dealt with swiftly in Henry's second parliament, which met from November to December 1487. Twenty-eight of them were attainted and their lands were confiscated.

Some historians view Stoke as the last battle of the Wars of the Roses. Certainly, Henry never again faced an army composed of his own subjects on English soil, although further rebellions did follow. Indeed Stoke could have been a second Bosworth, with Henry this time in the role of Richard III. What was most important was that Henry was victorious, and in spite of the added problem of foreign intervention. However, the fact that such a ridiculous scheme almost succeeded indicates that the country was still very unsettled and shows how fragile Henry's grasp on the crown was. It was no coincidence that on 25 November his wife, Elizabeth, and mother of his heir, was belatedly crowned queen. This was designed to unite the nation and to secure the goodwill of the people.

6 Perkin Warbeck, 1491–9

> **KEY ISSUE** How significant a danger to Henry VII were Perkin Warbeck and his supporters?

a) Origins of Warbeck's Rebellion

Further troubles arose for Henry in the autumn of 1491 when Perkin Warbeck, a 17-year-old from Tournai in France, arrived in Cork, Ireland, on the ship of his master, a Breton merchant. As he strolled around the town flaunting the silk wares of his master, his dignified bearing seems to have deeply impressed the townsfolk. They assumed that he must be the Earl of Warwick, as rumour was still rife about his whereabouts. Warbeck denied this, claiming instead to be Richard, Duke of York whose murder in the Tower was assumed but had never been proved. The known figures behind Warbeck were men of humble origin. However, Professor Chrimes believes that Warbeck's appearance in Ireland was 'no unpremeditated accident but was the first overt action in the unfolding of a definite plan'. He thinks that Charles VIII of France, and probably Margaret of Burgundy as well, wanted to use Warbeck to blackmail Henry if he became too anti-French over the Breton problem (see page 112). The only direct evidence available is Warbeck's own confession, which he made on the scaffold:

1   It is first to be known that I was born in the town of Tournai in
    Flanders, and my father's name is John Osbeck. I was led by my mother
    to Antwerp, for to learn Flemish in a house of a cousin of mine ... and
    then ... to board in a skinner's house that dwelled beside the house of
5   the English nation ... After this with a merchant of Middlesborough to
    service for to learn the language ... and then I went into Portugal in
    company of Sir Edward Brampton's wife and then I put myself in serv-
    ice with a Breton called Pregent Meno, who brought me with him into
    Ireland. Now when we were there arrived in the town of Cork, they of
10 the town (because I was arrayed with some kinds of cloths of silk of my
    master's) came unto me and threatened upon me that I should be the
    Duke of Clarence's son that was before time at Dublin ... and after this
    came unto me an Englishman and laid to me ... that they knew that I
    was King Richard's bastard son ... They advised me not to be afeared
15 but that I should take it upon me boldly ... so that they might be
    revenged on the King of England, and so against my will made me learn
    English and taught me what I should do and say. And after this they
    called me the Duke of York, second son to King Edward IV, because
    King Richard's bastard son was in the hands of the King of England ...
20 The French King sent an ambassador into Ireland ... to advertise me to
    come into France. And thence I went to France and from thence into

Flanders, and from Flanders into Ireland, and from Ireland into Scotland, and so into England.

b) Support for Warbeck

The conspiracy achieved international recognition from the predictable trouble spots of Ireland, Scotland and France. Charles VIII welcomed Warbeck at the French court and by the summer of 1492 approximately 100 English Yorkists had joined him in Paris. The Treaty of Étaples with France (see page 114) in November meant that he had to find a new refuge, so he fled to Flanders where he was accepted by Margaret of Burgundy as her nephew. In 1493 the extent of Henry's concern was shown when he temporarily broke off all trade with Flanders even though this jeopardised the cloth trade which was so important to the English economy. In the interim Warbeck found an even more influential patron than Margaret when Maximilian, the newly elected Holy Roman Emperor, recognised him as Richard IV in 1494. However, Maximilian did not have the resources available to finance an invasion of England. Charles VIII gave Henry a respite when he invaded Italy in 1494 and turned Europe's attention southwards away from the problems of the Tudor dynasty; Henry could now concentrate solely on the revolt without fear of European invasion as well. His intelligence network had informed him who was implicated both at home and abroad, and in the parliament of 1495 a number of acts of attainder were passed. The most important victim was Sir William Stanley, Henry's step-uncle and the man who had changed the course of the Battle of Bosworth. As Chamberlain of the king's household he was one of Henry's most trusted officials and Henry must have been disappointed and frightened by his betrayal. His execution showed that Henry would spare no traitor, however eminent. Lord Fitzwalter, his steward, was also executed. It appears that a supposed adherent of the conspiracy, Sir Robert Clifford, revealed vital names to the king. It is probable that Clifford was in Henry's service from the beginning, for he received a pardon and rewards for breaking the conspiracy.

c) The Failure of the Rebellion

The efficient work of Henry's agents and the king's swift reaction meant that Warbeck's attempted landing at Deal in July 1495 was a fiasco. He failed to gather sufficient local support and he set sail for Ireland, ruthlessly abandoning those of his men who had already gone ashore. He laid siege to the loyal town of Waterford for 11 days without success. He then departed for Scotland where he met with more encouragement, as the kings of Scotland always seized any opportunity to provoke their English counterparts. Therefore, James IV gave Warbeck refuge and support. It is difficult to be certain how far James was convinced by Warbeck, if at all, but he did go so far as to give him his cousin in marriage together with an annual pension of £1,200. These actions were enough to challenge Henry's government and to threaten the marriage alliance with Spain, between Catherine of Aragon and Arthur, Prince of Wales. King Ferdinand and Queen Isabella would not contemplate sending their daughter to marry the heir to a contested crown. Fortunately for Henry, the Scottish invasion of England was a disaster. Warbeck received no support south of the border and retreated, horrified at the manner in which the Scots raided and pillaged the countryside. James did not take advantage of the rebellion in Cornwall (see page 31) to attack again. Disillusioned with Warbeck, he thought that Henry's conciliatory offer of his eldest daughter, Margaret, in marriage was more to Scotland's long-term advantage. In September 1497 a seven-year truce was agreed at Ayton which was formalised in 1502 – the first full peace treaty with Scotland since 1328.

Warbeck himself eased the situation by returning to Ireland in July 1497, hoping for more success there. However, as he found that even Kildare (see page 60) was temporarily loyal to Henry, he set sail for the south-west of England hoping as a last resort to find support from this traditionally rebellious area. Again he was rudely disillusioned; having landed in Devon, he was driven out of Exeter and Taunton and only a few thousand countryfolk joined him. Within a fortnight it was all over, and Warbeck once again abandoned his followers. This time he fled to the sanctuary of Beaulieu Abbey in Hampshire. In August 1497 he was persuaded to give himself up and to make a full confession of his imposture. As a foreigner it would have been difficult at this stage to accuse him of treason under English law. Henry allowed him to remain at court with his young bride, but Warbeck was not content with this and foolishly ran away in 1498. He was recaptured, publicly humiliated by being forced to sit in the stocks twice, and was then imprisoned in the Tower. As for his wife, she remained at court and became a lady-in-waiting to the queen. It is difficult to determine the truth of what happened next. Whether he was manipulated by the king or actually did enter into a ridiculous plot with the Earl of Warwick who was still in the Tower, we shall never know. His exploits had certainly tried Henry's patience to the limit. In 1499 he was charged with trying to escape yet again and this time he was hanged. The Earl of Warwick was found guilty of treason and was executed a week later. It would indeed be ironic if Warbeck himself was used to get rid of Warwick. Innocuous as Warwick himself might have been, he was always there for others to manipulate and weave plots around. Very probably pressure from Spain forced Henry to act in this way. Ferdinand and Isabella wanted to ensure that their daughter was coming to a secure inheritance.

Warbeck maintained to the end that the plan to impersonate the Duke of York originated in Cork. However, there is evidence that he had learnt a great deal about the family of Edward IV from his former employer, Sir Edward Brampton, a converted Portuguese Jew, who had found favour at the Yorkist court. It is probable that his acceptance as pretender in Cork was part of a detailed plan and not a spontaneous reaction to public opinion. It is unlikely that he would have pursued his imposture for eight years had there not been more important figures behind him from the start. The most obvious person is Margaret of Burgundy, but there is no record of her meeting Warbeck before he left France in 1492. However, this does not mean that there had been no contact. Certainly in the absence of any genuine Yorkist claimant at liberty, supporting Warbeck would have seemed her best opportunity to dislodge Henry. She would also have been a valuable teacher on Yorkist affairs. Warbeck himself appears to have enjoyed the imposture, revelling in the attention he received at a variety of courts in Europe. However, it is unlikely that he actually convinced anyone of importance that he was genuine, except perhaps briefly James IV. Faithful Yorkists were prepared to back anyone in order to gain their revenge on Henry VII. Nevertheless, he did succeed in causing Henry eight years of considerable anxiety and expense that the king could well have done without.

7 Further Yorkist Threats, 1499–1506

> **KEY ISSUE** What impact did later Yorkist threats have on Henry's sense of insecurity?

On the death of Warwick, the chief Yorkist claimant to the throne was Edmund de la Pole, Earl of Suffolk, brother of the rebellious Earl of Lincoln who had died at Stoke. On the surface Suffolk appeared reconciled to Henry's rule, but there was underlying tension because the king refused to elevate him to the dukedom that his father had enjoyed. Quite suddenly in July 1499 Suffolk took flight to Guisnes, near Calais. Henry, fearing a further foreign-backed invasion by a rival claimant to his throne, persuaded him to return and he remained on amicable terms with the king until 1501. In that year he fled with his brother, Richard, to the court of Maximilian. What remained of the old Yorkist support once more gathered in Flanders. Fate seemed to be against Henry: in 1500 his third son, Edmund, died; in April 1502 his eldest son and heir, Arthur, followed him to the grave. The king's only male heir was now the 10-year-old Prince Henry, then surprisingly (in the light of his later considerable athleticism) not very strong. The fact that Henry now acted more ruthlessly than ever before reveals how insecure he must have felt. Suffolk's relations who remained in England were imprisoned and, in the parliament that met in January 1504, 51 men were attainted. This was the largest number condemned by any parliament during his reign. The most famous victim was Sir James Tyrell, once Constable of the Tower, and latterly Governor of Guisnes where Suffolk had temporarily rested. Before his execution, Tyrell conveniently confessed to murdering the two young princes, the sons of Edward IV, thus discouraging any further impostors. Henry seems to have been determined to pursue Suffolk to the end. This is not surprising if the report of an informer to the council about Suffolk's flight is to be believed. It tells of secret meetings at Calais to discuss Henry's successor:

> Some of them spake of my Lord of Buckingham, saying that he was a noble man and would be a royal ruler. Others there were that spake in likewise of yon traitor, Edmund de la Pole, but none of them spake of my Lord Prince.

Henry's luck seemed to change in 1506 when a storm caused Philip of Burgundy and his wife to take refuge off Weymouth. Exploiting the duke's weak position, Henry persuaded Philip to surrender Suffolk. He agreed to do so on condition that the earl's life would be spared. Henry kept his promise; Suffolk remained in the Tower until his execution by Henry VIII in 1513. Meanwhile, his brother, Richard de la Pole, remained at large in Europe trying in vain to muster support for his claim to the English throne. However, few Yorkists now remained and Henry was proving a strong and just monarch to those who were loyal. Richard was killed at the battle of Pavia in 1525 but he had never proved a serious threat to the Tudor monarchy.

So Henry could not have felt secure even after the deaths of Warbeck and Warwick in 1499. It was not until 1506 that the persistent threat of Yorkist claimants was, for the most part, eliminated. Even then the security of the dynasty rested on the heartbeat of his only son, Prince Henry. Queen Elizabeth had died in February 1503, and Henry's fear for the future of his dynasty is seen in the way he scoured the courts of Europe for a second wife.

8 Challenges to Henry's Rule: Rebellions in Yorkshire (1489) and Cornwall (1497)

> **KEY ISSUES** Why did rebellions occur in Yorkshire and Cornwall? How did Henry deal with them? What did he learn from them?

There were also challenges to Henry's rule within England. These rebellions stemmed not from dynastic causes but from the king's demands for money. However, they did influence the way in which Henry responded to the dynastic challenges and showed how delicate was the balance between public order and lawlessness.

Henry planned to go to the aid of Brittany (see page 112) and the parliament of 1489 granted him a subsidy of £100,000 to pay for it. The tax caused widespread resentment because it was raised in a new way, as a sort of income tax. The king appears to have received only £27,000 of the total granted. The tax was particularly badly received in Yorkshire which was suffering the after-effects of a bad harvest the previous summer. The people also resented the fact that the counties to the north of them were exempted from the tax because they were expected to defend the country from the Scots. Henry Percy, Earl of Northumberland, put their case to the king, but Henry refused to negotiate. When the Earl returned north with the news, he was murdered, presumably by malcontents. The king has sometimes been thought to have been behind this murder as one of the leaders, John à Chambre, had been one of his ardent supporters ever since Bosworth – despite the fact that Chambre was now captured and executed. However, Northumberland was not popular in the area because he had supported the tax, and a more likely culprit was the embittered Sir John Egremont, subsequent leader of the rebellion and an illegitimate member of the Percy family. The Earl of Surrey finally defeated the rebels outside York and Egremont escaped to Flanders. The king travelled north to issue a pardon to most of the prisoners as a gesture of conciliation, but he failed to collect any more of this tax. He faced no more trouble in the north because the new Earl of Northumberland was only a minor and a ward of the crown. To further ensure this Henry appointed the Earl of Surrey as his Lieutenant in this area. Surrey had no vested interest in the north and his loyalty was guaranteed because the restoration of his own estates rested on his success here.

It was another request for money that ignited a rebellion in Cornwall. In January 1497 parliament voted a heavy tax to finance an expedition north to resist the projected invasion of James IV and Warbeck. The Cornish, who were traditionally independent, refused to contribute to the defence of the northern part of the kingdom to suppress an invasion which offered little threat to them. Holinshed's *Chronicle*, first published in 1571, sets out the causes of the grievances of the rebels as follows:

1 These unruly people, the Cornishmen, inhabiting in a barren country and unfruitful, at the first sore repined that they should be so grievously taxed and burdened by the King's council ... Flammock and Joseph [the local leaders] exhorted the common people to put on harness and not
5 be afeared to follow them in that quarrel, promising not to hurt any creature, but only to see them punish that procured such exactions to be laid on the people, without any reasonable cause, as under the colour of a little trouble with the Scots, which (since they were withdrawn home) they took to be well quieted and appeased ...

In May the rebels set out from Bodmin and marched through the western counties, acquiring their only leader of any significance, the impoverished Lord Audley, at Wells. On 16 June, about 15,000 strong, they reached the outskirts of London and encamped on Blackheath. In the meantime, the king had diverted his forces south under Lord Daubeney. Holinshed continues:

> 1 The city was in great fear ... the rebels were encamped so near the city, every man getting himself to harness and placing themselves some at the gates some on the walls, so that no part was undefended. But the King delivered the city of that fear ... There were slain of the rebels
> 5 which fought and resisted, above 2,000 men and taken prisoners an infinite number, and among them the blacksmith [Joseph] and the other chief captains, which were shortly after put to death.

Another English chronicler, John Stowe, quotes different statistics about the Battle of Blackheath. His *Annals of England* was first published in 1592:

> Lord Daubeney came into the field with his company, and without long fighting on 22 June the Cornishmen were overcome ... There were slain of the rebels about 3,000 and taken of them about 1,500 ... The King wanted of all his number about 300 men, which were slain.

Historians now estimate that about 1,000 rebels were killed in the battle and that the rest swiftly fled. Only Audley and the two original local leaders were executed. Despite the fact that the rising had been defeated, it was worrying that the rebels had been able to march as far as Kent before facing any opposition. Henry had been directing his attention towards Scotland and Warbeck and, as the Cornish rising was an independent rebellion, unconnected with any Yorkist conspiracy, he had not responded to it early on. The rebellion hardly endangered his throne, but it had illustrated that he could not afford a serious campaign against Scotland. Henry now attempted to come to terms with James.

The rebellions in Yorkshire and Cornwall were not in themselves important but they complicated other problems. They affected the way in which Henry handled the impostors as they showed that the country was not prepared to finance a major war in defence of the Tudor regime. Henry's diplomatic skills were tested to the full in the challenges he faced to his throne. He was fortunate in that rebellion was regionalised; many of his subjects were not inclined to take up arms, less because of their devotion to the Tudor dynasty than their apathy towards a civil conflict that had lasted far too long already. At times he had to negotiate carefully and when there was no other choice he had to resort to force. Henry himself seems to have preferred to fight only when absolutely necessary. This was slower but cheaper and, therefore, preferable to both the king and his subjects. As time went on the stability that Henry was working towards led many to be content with his style of government.

9 Conclusion: When did Henry feel Secure on his Throne?

> **KEY ISSUE** What factors contributed to making Henry secure on his throne?

Henry never felt entirely secure on his throne. Even after the capture of Edmund de la Pole in 1506, his brother, Richard, was still roaming Europe, although with little success. The king's only direct male heir was the young Prince Henry. He faced rebellions from his own subjects over demands for money which showed that he could only rely on their loyalty to a limited extent. The challenge from former Yorkists, particularly the Earl of Suffolk, was unnerving, especially after they had sworn loyalty to the new regime. Worse still was the threat from the pretenders, Simnel and Warbeck, because of their entanglement with foreign powers and the consequent fear of invasion.

It is easy to overlook how great these dangers were when reviewing the successful policies Henry pursued in other areas of government – finance, trade and the restoration of law and order. We must be careful not to forget the unstable background against which these successes were achieved. Henry learnt his lesson from Lincoln's betrayal in 1487 and implemented a more sophisticated system of well-paid and well-placed agents which enabled him to detect Warbeck's conspiracy in the early stages. The king was not vindictive towards his opponents and saw the advantage of using attainders against them rather than the hangman's rope. His two most notable victims were Sir William Stanley and the Earl of Warwick. Stanley's only crime was in agreeing not to oppose Warbeck if he were really the son of Edward IV. He was executed because of his closeness to the king, where treachery of any type could not be tolerated, and his death acted as a deliberate warning to others. Warwick probably died innocent of any crime except being born of Yorkist blood. After enduring the exploits of Simnel and Warbeck, Henry must have felt that he was too dangerous a temptation to others for him to be allowed to live. It is a credit to Henry's clear, decisive judgement and diplomatic skill that he managed to hand on his throne intact to his son, when the previous three kings of England had failed to do so.

Working on Chapter 2

You need to be clear in your own mind how Henry VII secured his throne and how he established his dynasty. The period before 1485 is only of peripheral importance so you should concentrate on events after the battle of Bosworth. Study the summary diagram carefully, it will provide you with the framework for what you need to write. You will notice that securing his throne was a short-term aim which he largely accomplished during 1485–86. Here your notes should concentrate on how Henry VII strengthened his position in these crucial first two years. Firmly establishing his dynasty was an altogether more protracted struggle covering the period from 1487 until 1506. Here you need to consider why Henry felt so vulnerable and how he met the challenges to his rule.

Answering structured and essay questions on Chapter 2

If the paper you are sitting is made up of two-part structured questions you may find that they are worded similarly to the following:

a) Explain briefly why Henry VII's accession to the throne was challenged. (6 marks)

b) How successfully did Henry VII suppress the challenges of the Pretenders, Lambert Simnel and Perkin Warbeck? (9 marks)

In order to answer such questions successfully you need first to seek out and identify the key words. In this case they are a) challenged and b) suppress. Once you have done this you should consider the following advice for each of the questions.

a) The examiner is seeking to test your historical knowledge and understanding, therefore you should begin by clearly establishing the fact that it was Henry's 'right' to the throne that was being challenged. Your answer should then proceed by citing relevant factors such as the attitude of the nobility and disaffected elements, the nature of the claims raised by pretenders and the means employed by Henry to cement his battlefield victory.

b) Here your ability to evaluate and analyse is also being tested. Therefore it is important to remember that marks will be awarded both for the factual content of your answer and for the analytical skills you display. Your answer might consist of the following elements: military force; attitude to/treatment of the claims of the Pretenders, treatment also of them following their challenges to Henry; shrewd diplomatic dealings with

Summary Diagram
Establishing the Tudor Dynasty

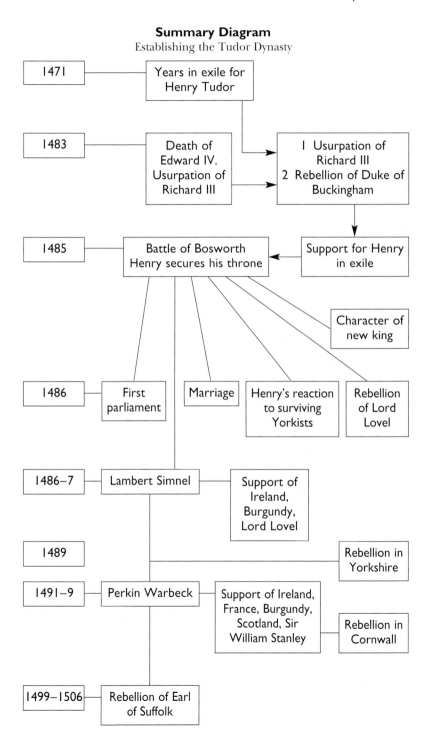

neighbouring states/rulers tempted to afford Pretenders recognition and support.

In order to gain between 6–9 marks your answer must clearly demonstrate an understanding of these factors and not merely be a narrative response focusing on details of actual suppression.

Essays will be a central part of the way you study throughout your course and in the examinations you will use them to show your historical knowledge, skills and understanding. Before writing an essay it is essential to draw up a plan. The amount of detail in a plan will vary from student to student. For some it will only be a series of words or phrases which provide the key to each paragraph, while for others it will be a comprehensive set of notes indicating the direction and shape the essay is to take. Neither approach is wrong. It is up to you to find the most effective method for yourself. In essay planning, practice makes perfect!

Every essay should contain an introduction, a middle and a conclusion. The middle will be the argument – the main body of the essay – and will be by far the longest part of it. The introduction, particularly the first sentence, is often the hardest to compose. Remember that the introduction introduces the argument. It does far more than merely set the scene. It establishes the way the essay will develop. Think of the essay as a journey and the introduction as the time when you state which route you will be taking, and perhaps what might be seen on route. As you have now given your directions, you cannot change course midway. The introduction is the first thing that the examiner will read and it is important to make a good impression at the beginning!

A common problem facing students, particularly at the beginning of their course, is learning how to structure an essay. It is a good idea to set a limit to the essay so that you feel in control and don't degenerate into filling up the paper with waffle. Try the 'seven point rule' whereby you identify seven major points that are vital to answering the question asked. Then select the information that illustrates the points you are making. Each point should equal one paragraph.

It would be a mistake to regard this chapter in isolation or to dismiss it merely as background. Some questions on Henry VII demand an overall view of his reign in which it is important to put the challenges to the throne into perspective, and we shall discuss these in Chapter 7. However, questions do occur on how Henry VII secured the throne. A typical question of this type is:

I. Why, and how, did Henry VII not only replace the Yorkists on the throne of England but finally ensure that there would be no Yorkist return to the throne?

When questions begin with a Why?, construct a plan consisting of points beginning with 'because'. Such a plan might begin with a first point: 'Because of Richard III's unexpected usurpation and the nature of his rule.' However, do not forget the equally important instruction How? ie. how did he do it. The examiner will expect you to explain the means by which Henry not only replaced the Yorkists on the throne but ensured they would never return.

When writing your essay, expand each of these points into full paragraphs, including plenty of detail to reinforce your argument. In developing the first point, for instance, you could refer to the unsettled nature of the country after Richard seized the throne and give examples of ways in which his rule was unpopular.

Now for the conclusion. Like the introduction this is a vital part of the essay because you are leaving the examiner with the final impression of what you have written. Some of the best conclusions are short. Your aim should be to summarise clearly your main argument and to show how and why it agrees with or differs from the essay title.

Another typical question is:

2. How serious was the threat posed to Henry VII by the pretenders to the throne?

The key words here are 'How serious'. It is easy to make the mistake of writing a narrative of each of the challenges to Henry's throne and you must not do this. Instead you must establish the dangers that each presented and assess how serious they were from Henry's point of view. For example, you need to consider the support that the pretenders attracted, both from inside and outside the country. Look at how Henry reacted to them and how easily or otherwise he overcame them. To ensure that you keep to the question, try to assess at the end of each paragraph how serious was the threat of the point you are making.

Answering source-based questions on Chapter 2

Working with contemporary sources of evidence has become an integral part of study at GCSE, A/S and A level. To be successful you need to build on the skills learnt at GCSE. You must begin by comprehending the content of the source, after which you should analyse the information by breaking it down into component parts depending on the questions asked. As you were required to do at GCSE you can expect to be asked to compare and contrast sources, to interpret their content by inference and deduction, and to evaluate by assessing their usefulness and reliability. You will be given an opportunity to practise each of these skills when using the study guides in this book.

In the majority of cases the primary sources you will encounter have been translated into modern English but this does not mean that they will be easy to understand. The language and written style can often prove very difficult. The sources printed in the profile on Jasper Tudor will give you some idea of what fifteenth-century English was like and of the problems of translating fifteenth-century Welsh into twentieth-century English! In your own words try to explain their meaning.

1. The Personality of Henry VII

Read the extracts from Polydore Vergil's *Anglica Historia* and John Fisher's funeral oration on page 19, and Francis Bacon's *History of the Reign of King Henry VII* on page 19. Also look carefully at the portrait of Henry by Sittow on the front cover. Answer the following questions:

a) Which of the characteristics mentioned in Vergil's description of Henry do you think were the most admirable in a king at this time? Give reasons for your answer. *(4 marks)*
b) Compare Sittow's portrait of Henry with Vergil's description. In what ways do they i) agree and ii) disagree about his appearance? Explain the differences. *(5 marks)*
c) Which of these sources is likely to be the most accurate? Explain your answer. *(6 marks)*

2. Perkin Warbeck's Confession

Read the extract taken from Perkin Warbeck's confession on pages 26–7. Answer the following questions:

a) What impression do you gain of Warbeck's character and personality from the events he recounts of his early life in lines 1–9? *(3 marks)*
b) How does Warbeck account for his portrayal as the 'Duke of Clarence's son' in line 12? *(2 marks)*
c) Who might the 'Englishman' in line 13 have been? *(1 mark)*
d) Give reasons for the frequent comings and goings of Warbeck in lines 21–23. *(4 marks)*
e) How reliable do you think this account is? Consider the circumstances in which it was written. *(5 marks)*

3. The Cornish Rebellion of 1497

Read the passages about this rebellion from Holinshed's *Chronicle* and John Stowe's *Annals of England* on page 32. Answer the following questions:

a) What reason does Holinshed give for the outbreak of rebellion in Cornwall? *(2 marks)*

b) Consider the tone of this extract. What impression does the author give of the rebels' behaviour? *(4 marks)*

c) In what ways do the two extracts differ in their reports of the results and aftermath of the Battle of Blackheath? *(4 marks)*

d) How useful would these extracts be to the historian as evidence of the Cornish Rebellion? *(5 marks)*

3 The Establishment of Good Governance

POINTS TO CONSIDER

This chapter explains the framework of government at this time, and sets out the ways in which Henry VII attempted to re-establish law and order after the Wars of the Roses. As you read this chapter you should note the problems Henry faced and the methods he used to overcome them. Concentrate particularly on identifying where he pursued the same policy as his Yorkist predecessors (continuity), and where he introduced his own ideas (change). Consider his motives and the results of his actions. You should think carefully about the degree of Henry's success – in what ways was he successful and in what ways not?

KEY DATES

1485 Meeting of first parliament, in which Henry's claim to the royal title was ratified.

1487 Act passed for the setting up of a tribunal to enforce law and order.

1493 Council in Wales and the Marches was re-established.

1494 Sir Edward Poynings appointed Lord Deputy of Ireland. He arranged the passage of what became known as Poynings' Law. This decreed that Irish parliaments could only be called and pass laws with the prior approval of the king.

c. 1495 Council Learned in the Law established and entrusted with the task of defending the King's rights as a feudal landlord.

1504 Sir Richard Empson appointed head of the Council Learned. He ran it with ruthless efficiency, imposing financial penalties on the nobility.

1 Background

> **KEY ISSUE** How did people of the late middle ages view society and their part in it?

a) The Theory of Obligation

The maintenance of law and order was vital to the survival of a medieval king. Rulers were seen as God's deputies on earth, the temporal power, acting as guardians of His people. Therefore, any threat to the internal peace and security of the nation was interpreted as an indication of God's displeasure with His deputy, whose authority might be seriously challenged as a result. Rebellion or any type of civil unrest was abhorrent to most people from nobleman to peasant because, as Sir Thomas Elyot wrote, 'Where there is any lack of order needs must be perpetual conflict'. This meant that the worst fear for most people was an outbreak of general anarchy. The late middle ages is, of course, littered with examples of this type of unrest: the Peasants' Revolt in 1381 against the poll tax, the conflict over the crown in the middle of the fifteenth century, and the rebellion in Cornwall in 1497, again stemming mainly from the ill-feeling caused by what was regarded to be an unjustified tax. On all these occasions resentment built up slowly and people only took up arms as a last resort. There was little violence for the sake of violence. Thus, although the recent Wars of the Roses acted as a warning to Henry of how an incompetent or unscrupulous monarch could be overthrown, they also showed him that his subjects would quickly return to obedience if he proved capable of asserting the right degree of authority. *A Mirror for Magistrates*, edited by William Baldwin, was published in 1559 and reprinted six times in the following 18 years. It conveys the contemporary idea of God punishing those who rebelled against their prince:

1 Full little know we wretches what we do
   When we presume our Princes to resist.
   We war with God against His glory too,
   That placeth in His office whom He list.
5 Therefore was never traitor yet but missed
   The mark he shot at, and came to fearful end,
   Nor ever shall till God be forced to bend.

b) The Great Chain of Being

It is also important to remember a concept known as 'The Great Chain of Being' when trying to understand how Tudor society operated. This was the belief that every man was born to a specific place in the strict hierarchy of society and had a duty to remain there. It is clearly expressed by Sir John Fortescue, one of Henry VII's Chief Justices:

1 God created as many different kinds of things as He did creatures, so
   that there is no creature which does not differ in some respect superior
   or inferior to all the rest. So that from the highest angel down to the
   lowest of his kind there is absolutely not found an angel that has not a
5 superior and inferior; nor from man down to the meanest worm is
   there any creature which is not in some respect superior to one creature and inferior to another. So that there is nothing which the bond of
   order does not embrace.

The Great Chain of Being meant co-operation between men of differing ranks, not mere subjugation to your social superior. However, it did emphasise that those in authority held their power for the good of those below them, and subject to those above them.

The Wars of the Roses had temporarily upset this natural order of society with the crown being fought over by rival factions. This lowered the status of the monarchy. It was nobles who had profited most from this, seizing the opportunity to take the law into their own hands and acting as quasi-kings in their own localities. Although they had always tried to have the last word in their own area, they now took this a step further, using their servants and retainers as private armies to settle their petty quarrels and to make or unmake kings on the battlefields of the recent civil wars. In 1485 it was this class over whom Henry had to assert his authority if he was to restore the dignity and authority of the monarchy. His problem, according to one historian, S.T. Bindoff, was 'how to suppress the magnates' abuse of their power while preserving the power itself'. A great nobleman had the power to provoke disorder and even revolt, but he could also quell rebellion and act as a mediator between the people and central government. Henry hoped that by imposing his will by ruthless impartiality the nobles might learn to accept that their position was one of obedience, loyalty and service to the crown, and if this was achieved the rest of his subjects would follow suit, as the nobility were the natural leaders of society. In this context it can be argued that his reign marks the end of an independent feudal nobility and the beginning of a service nobility. Therefore, the purpose of this chapter is, in part, to investigate the role played by Henry in the transformation of the nature and function of the nobility, but also to examine the means he had at his disposal for imposing his will, the methods he employed, and the degree of success he achieved.

2 The Nobility

> **KEY ISSUE** What was the nature of Henry's relationship with his nobility?

a) Size of the Nobility

It is a common misconception that most nobles were killed during the Wars of the Roses, and that Henry therefore only had a small upper class to bring under control. This has been disproved by recent research which has shown that the direct male lines of peerage families failed no faster in the mid-fifteenth century than at any other time in the later middle ages. In fact, there was always a high extinction rate, either due to death in battle or because peers failed to leave sons to succeed them. On average in the later middle ages in every 25-year period a quarter of noble lines died out and were replaced by new families. What Henry did to make his task of bringing the nobility to heel easier was to keep the peerage small by limiting the number of new lords that he created. This was unusual and in direct contrast to the policies of Edward IV and Henry VIII in whose reigns the nobility grew significantly in size. Henry VII deliberately refrained from making new creations for three reasons: firstly, a limited noble class was easier to control; secondly, he so rarely elevated anyone to the upper echelons of society that it was regarded as a particularly prized honour and distinction when it did happen; and thirdly – and, from Henry's point of view, most importantly – the grant of a title might involve the king in expenditure on quite a large scale. A title often brought with it large estates and, as these were usually granted from crown lands, the creation of new peers resulted in a loss of income for the king. If titles were handed out on a large scale, it could mean quite a considerable drop in the rents that the crown received.

Whereas Edward IV created nine new Earls, Henry created only three – his step-father, Lord Stanley, who became Earl of Derby; Philibert de Chandee who, in recognition of his military skill as captain of his mercenary troops at Bosworth, became Earl of Bath; and, lastly, Sir Edward Courtenay who was vested with the title of Earl of Devon, left extinct by the death of his cousin John at the battle of Tewkesbury in 1471. Even after Bosworth, Sir William Stanley and Sir Rhys ap Thomas, to whom Henry owed so much for his victory, were not made peers. However his uncle, Jasper Tudor, who had acted as his guardian and mentor through childhood and exile, was elevated from Earl of Pembroke (restored to him in 1485) to Duke of Bedford. Other than that, he created only one marquess (briefly), one viscount, and eight barons during the remainder of his reign, as compared with Edward's two viscounts and 13 barons. Of Henry's creations only three were genuinely new peerages which needed to be accompanied by grants of land. The peerage consequently shrank from around 62 in 1485 to about 42 in 1509 as new creations failed to keep pace with the number of noble families that died out through natural and, in some cases, unnatural extinction. According to one historian, T.B. Pugh, 'Royal intervention was far more effective than the failure of male heirs in diminishing the group of great magnate families'. He cites the case of Sir Walter Herbert whose claim to his late elder brother's Earldom of Huntington was ignored by Henry who thereby allowed the title to lapse. The fact that Walter was well known to the king, having been brought up with him at Raglan when the young Henry was put in the care of Herbert's father, the Yorkist Earl of Pembroke, counted for little.

Henry found a useful alternative to the bestowal of a peerage on his loyal subjects, namely the award of Order of the Garter. This was an ancient honour which was in the gift of the crown but which involved it in no financial obligations, and 37 of Henry's closest followers (including peers) received this privilege during his reign. Among those honoured were Sir William Stanley and Sir Rhys ap

Thomas but, whereas the latter embraced the award with enthusiasm, Stanley considered it scant reward for his good service.

b) Over-mighty Subjects

Henry was fortunate in his handling of the nobility that he faced fewer of the over-mighty nobles who had so troubled Edward IV. One reason for this was his lack of close male relatives; whereas Edward had had to cope with two powerful brothers, the Dukes of Clarence and Gloucester, Henry had no close male blood relatives. He did have step-brothers but he felt little obligation towards them. The other reason was the king's cautious policy in rewarding his followers. The lands that came to the crown from extinct peerage families were not given away again. They were mostly retained, particularly the great estates that were acquired from the extinct Yorkist families of Warwick, Clarence and Gloucester. Henry also controlled the marriages of his nobles, carefully ensuring that leading magnates did not link themselves to great heiresses in order to create new and dangerous power blocs. He was able to do this because, as their feudal lord, his permission was necessary for their marriages to take place. For example, when Katherine Wydevill married her third husband, Sir Richard Wingfield, without royal licence, a punitive fine of £2,000 – equivalent to the annual income of several hundred ordinary people – was imposed. That she had once been the wife of Henry's uncle, Jasper Tudor, Duke of Bedford, was never allowed to come between the king and his duty.

Some of these over-mighty subjects, such as the Percy Earls of Northumberland and the Stafford Dukes of Buckingham, did of course remain from the past. But such families were kept under close surveillance. For example, although the Duke of Buckingham came into his inheritance at the age of seven in 1485, Henry did not allow him to take possession of his property until 1498. Meanwhile, the king acted as his guardian and retained the profits of his estates. The Duke was not allowed to receive the benefits of his estates until he had proved his loyalty to the Tudor dynasty. The Earl of Northumberland, who was murdered in 1489, left his 10-year-old son as heir. But he was not allowed to take possession of his property until 1499 – again, not until the king was convinced of his loyalty. Even closely-related famil-ies with the potential to become over-mighty, like the Stanley Earls of Derby, were kept firmly in check. Fearful of the family's growing wealth and power, the core of which had been given them by Henry, in 1506 the king took the opportunity to fine Bishop Stanley, his step-brother, the huge sum of £245,680 for illicit retaining. In an act cal-culated to bring to heel his young nephew, the second Earl Stanley, payment of part of the fine, over £1,800, was made his responsibility. So, partly through good fortune and partly through a carefully thought out policy, the greater magnates posed less of a threat to Henry than they had in previous reigns.

c) Did Henry deliberately try to limit the Power of the Nobility?

Traditional interpretations of Henry's reign argued that he quickly recognised the potential danger of the nobility and deliberately set out to quell them. As evidence of this, the way in which the king thrust the nobility from their traditional advisory role on the council and replaced them with professional lawyers and administrators was cited. This is now seen to be exaggerated and to some extent inaccurate. In fact, the 'truth' of Henry's relationship with the nobility is very much more complex and is the subject of continuing historical debate. More recently, historians have tended to emphasise the fact that although Henry was suspicious of the nobility, because he did not know the majority of them, having been brought up in Wales and France, he was not pursuing a consciously anti-noble policy. It has even been suggested that because Henry 'did not know the élite as he had not been brought up with them at court' that his suspicion of the nobility bordered on 'paranoia', but this is probably going too far. Two of his closest companions were the Earls of Oxford and Shrewsbury, neither of whom, unlike the Dukes of Bedford and Buckingham, Viscount Welles and the Earl of Derby, was related to him.

'Contrary to received myth, Henry had a court with courtiers and lavish court spectacle' (C. Carpenter) and many of those who attended the king in his court were his nobility. These included lesser nobles such as Barons Daubeney and Willoughby de Broke and great magnates such as the Earls of Shrewsbury and Essex. This suggests that Henry was frequently in their company, that he got to know them and that he came to rely on them, particularly when he wished to impress foreign visitors and ambassadors. In addition, they made a major contribution to court pageantry and entertainment. On the other hand, one of the main reasons why Henry kept some of the nobility close to him at court was so that he could keep an eye on them. So, according to one of his most notorious agents, Edmund Dudley, 'he was much sett to have the persons in his danger at his pleasure'. It is clear also that the nobility involved themselves in the political dynamics of Henry's court. Court faction and political infighting, so much a feature of the reigns of Henry VI and Edward IV, took on a more significant and sinister role in Henry's last years. Two notable victims of court politics are thought to have been Thomas Grey, second Marquess of Dorset, suspicion of whom had been 'stirred in Henry' by others, and George Neville, Baron Abergavenny, who was the only nobleman to suffer the public disgrace of being tried, fined and imprisoned for illegal retaining. It seems that, whereas Henry mistrusted many of his nobility, he did favour a few. This imbalance may have contributed to feuding at court.

Like his predecessors, he recognised the nobles' importance to him in controlling the provinces in the absence of a standing army and of an adequate police force. He never attempted to interfere with their authority in the localities and they continued to dominate local government. Moreover, Henry continued the medieval practice of granting the overlordship of the outlying, and therefore more disturbed, areas of his kingdom to the greater magnates as a gesture of goodwill. So, despite his dubious support at Bosworth, Henry Percy, the Earl of Northumberland, was released from captivity after only a few weeks and was regranted the wardenship of the north of England. On his death in 1489 the king made his own three-year-old son, Prince Arthur, warden but with another magnate, the Earl of Surrey, exercising real control as lieutenant. On the other hand, it has been argued that Henry's lack of instinctive trust in his 'natural partners', the nobility, may well have led to the undermining of local government. The problem, according to C. Carpenter, seems to have been Henry's 'lack of judgement over how to delegate and to whom'. The result in some areas, such as the north-west and midlands, was feuding among the king's servants and a general degeneration in law and order.

d) Henry's Attitude towards Patronage

One aspect of Henry's treatment of the nobility that was new was his attitude towards patronage (the distribution of royal favours). Unlike his predecessors he did not try to buy the loyalty of the nobility through the use of patronage. He was as circumspect in this as he was over the distribution of titles. The criterion he used in selecting those to receive royal favour was good and staunch service to the crown over a substantial period of time. This meant that it was not necessarily members of the nobility who fell into this category. The beneficiaries of Henry's generosity were quite simply valuable servants of the Tudor government. Some were peers, such as Jasper Tudor, the Duke of Bedford; the Earl of Oxford in return for his military support; and George Talbot, Earl of Shrewsbury, a notable administrator; but many were not. Edmund Dudley, the Sussex lawyer, who rose to become one of Henry's most trusted advisers, was not made a peer, but he 'used his title of King's Councillor as proudly as any peerage'. Loyalty and ability were Henry's sole requirements in his most important servants; patronage had to be earned, it was not an automatic privilege of the upper class.

The career of Thomas Howard, Earl of Surrey, illustrates clearly how Henry was prepared to forget past misdemeanours if their perpetrators subsequently performed loyally for him. The earl's father had enjoyed the title of Duke of Norfolk, an honour bestowed on him by Richard III, and he had died fighting for his king at Bosworth. After Henry's accession, the earl was imprisoned in the Tower and both he and his father were attainted. However, Surrey was released in 1489 and put in charge of maintaining law and order in the north, probably because he had impressed the king by turning down the chance to escape from the Tower during the Simnel plot. The attainder was revoked and his title was restored, but Henry only returned some of his lands – those of his wife and earlier ancestors. After his success in suppressing the Yorkshire rebellion he was given back the nucleus of the Howard estates but, in spite of his continued loyalty to the crown, he never received back all his father's lands. The ducal title was also denied him and Henry kept this final prize to ensure his loyalty to the end. It was not until 1513 that Henry VIII finally rewarded Surrey with the dukedom for his leading role in defeating the Scots at Flodden. Henry frequently used acts of attainder in this 'cat and mouse' way to punish recalcitrant magnates. After a period of time he would often arrange for parliament to revoke them, but he would only gradually restore the confiscated lands as rewards for actions of particular loyalty and support. Lesser nobles were sometimes forced to pay large sums of money for such reversals because they did not have as much to offer the king in terms of service or influence in their particular localities.

e) Financial Threats imposed on the Nobility

Henry also used financial threats to strengthen royal authority and curb the power of the nobility, particularly where he was suspicious of an individual but could not prove treason. In such cases he manipulated the existing system of bonds and recognisances for good behaviour to his advantage. These were written agreements in which a person who offended the king in a particular way was forced either to pay up front, or, like present-day bail, promised to pay a certain sum of money as security for their future good behaviour. This technique, sometimes with conditions attached, such as the carrying out of a certain duty, was used with all the élite classes as a method of ensuring their loyalty. Henry used the system not only to act as a financial threat against potentially disloyal magnates but to raise much-needed revenue for the crown. The sums stipulated in these agreements ranged from £400 for a relatively insignificant person to £10,000 for a peer.

As with his policy over acts of attainder, the greater the magnate, the more likely Henry was to bring him under this type of financial pressure. Typical was the case of Lord Dacre who was forced to make a bond of £2,000 for his loyalty in 1506 which Henry could repeal 'at his gracious pleasure'. When the Earl of Kent was deeply in debt to the king in 1507 he had to be 'seen daily once in the day within the king's house' to ensure that he had not bolted! Neither were spiritual lords exempt from such treatment. The Bishop of Worcester had to promise to pay £2,000 if his loyalty was ever in question, as well as agreeing not to leave the country. But the most important noble to suffer in this way was Edward IV's step-son, the Marquess of Dorset. The king had believed him to be implicated in the Simnel plot and, after further treachery in 1491, his friends signed bonds totalling £10,000 as a promise of his good behaviour. When Henry was planning the invasion of France in 1492 he even went so far as to take the Marquess's son as hostage in case he seized this opportunity to rebel again. Towards the end of his reign, Henry even requested recognisances from those taking up new appointments. These would not be forfeited if they performed their duties in an efficient, loyal and honest manner. For example, the Captain of Calais had to promise £40,000.

This policy of Henry's has been much commented upon, not so much because of its novelty but because of the extent to which he used it as a way of curbing the political power of the nobility. Use of such recognisances can be found throughout the fifteenth century but other kings employed them more haphazardly and infrequently. However, for Henry they were an integral part of his policy for controlling the nobility by threatening financial ruin to any family which dared to offend him. This did not mean that Henry was consciously pursuing a policy that was anti-noble. He appreciated the significance of the magnates to the fabric of society, but he was determined that any individual who chose to abuse his position should be firmly restrained. All the lords bound in such a fashion were guilty of offences that deserved large fines, but Henry showed that he was prepared to waive part of this if they would accept conditions which left them partly at his mercy. One of the reasons why Henry is accused of bleeding the nobility in later years is because during this period Empson and Dudley were in control of the Council Learned (see page 58) which was responsible for exacting such fines. It was possibly because of their non-noble origins that these two ministers were particularly unpopular, but it was more probably because they carried out their duties with such energy and efficiency. This degree of loyal service was what Henry expected from all his subjects, rich and poor alike. The nobility suffered most during his reign because they posed the greatest threat to his authority and to the security of his dynasty.

3 Retaining

> **KEY ISSUES** What was Henry's attitude towards retaining? What action did he take over it?

a) What was Livery and Maintenance?

One of the most serious problems that late medieval kings had to contend with was that of illegal retaining (the employment of private armies), often referred to as livery and maintenance. Livery was the giving of a uniform or badge to a follower, and maintenance was the protection of a follower's interests. This was a common practice whereby great lords recruited those of lesser status as their servants or followers to help advance their affairs (by force of arms if necessary) and to increase their prestige. They were given a uniform on which was emblazoned their master's crest or coat of arms showing whom they served. Kings had permitted this practice to exist because it could help the magnate control his particular locality and provided a quick and efficient way of raising an army, both of which were important to the king. Apart from these obvious uses, it was felt to be only natural that a nobleman should be attended by a retinue of men of respectable social status. However, the recent civil wars had shown that these retainers could also play an important part in lawlessness at both local and national levels, and could be used as an effective force against the king. Retainers could also be used as armed forces to threaten those who opposed their master. Interferences of this kind occurred not just to settle the lord's disputes but also those of his servants. This was because the lords had obligations to their followers. In the indenture (agreement) of retainder they undertook to be good lords to their men. However, it was originally meant to be based on principles of honour and mutual respect, with a lord accepting the responsibility of advancing and protecting the interests of his client, but not where they clashed with the law! Thus maintenance was now all too often abused, with nobles frequently going beyond the bounds of 'good lordship'.

b) Edward IV's Legislation against Retaining

Edward IV's parliament of 1468 had passed a statute prohibiting retaining except for domestic servants, estate officials and legal advisers. However, this law was largely ineffectual because it allowed the continuance of retaining for 'lawful service'. Therefore, during Edward's reign nobles continued to maintain their retinues using the excuse that they were doing so within the existing framework of the law. Indeed, as many as 64 new indentures of retainder for one nobleman still survive from the years 1469–82 alone. Historians now conclude that Edward intended this statute merely as 'a public relations exercise' and passed it to soothe the fears of the House of Commons but with no intention of strictly adhering to it.

ı Indenture of Retainder, 1481
    This indenture made the twenty fifth day of April the twenty first year
    of the reign of King Edward IV between William Hastings, knight, Lord
    Hastings, on the one part, and Ralph Longford, esquire, on the other
5 part, witnesseth that the said Ralph agreeth, granteth, and by these
    present indentures bindeth him to the said lord to be his retained servant during his life, and to him to do faithful and true service, and the

part of the same lord take against all men in peace and war with as many persons defensibly arrayed as the same Ralph can or may make at all
10 times that said lord will command him, at the said lord's costs and charges, saving the allegiance which the same Ralph oweth to the king our sovereign lord and to the prince. And the said lord granteth to the said Ralph to be his good and favourable lord and him aid and support in his right according to the law. In witness hereof the foresaid parties
15 to these present indentures have interchangeably set their seals and signs manual the day and year aforesaid.

c) Henry VII's Attitude towards Retaining

Henry VII openly condemned retaining at the beginning of his reign and two laws were passed against it in 1487 and 1504. Yet historians have differed in their opinions of the king's real attitude towards this practice. Originally they identified this as one of Henry's most astute and innovative policies. However, as more research was undertaken into the fifteenth century, it appeared that he was merely continuing what he understood to be the policy of his Yorkist predecessor – of limiting the amount of retaining rather than attempting to eliminate it altogether. Certainly, he still relied on the nobles' armies to protect the interests of the crown in times of emergency. In 1486 it was the Earl of Northumberland's force which rescued the king from ambush in Yorkshire, and the army that he led across the Channel to France in 1492 was raised from many of his lords' retinues. Further, the wording of Henry's statutes against retaining appeared to support the contention that he did not really intend to stop the practice completely. The acts of 1487 and 1504 did little more than repeat the statute of 1468. However, the most up-to-date research now concludes that Henry's attitude towards retaining was actually quite different from Edward IV's. Historians who put forward this argument begin by referring to the first months of the reign when the king forced the members of both Houses of Parliament to swear that they would not retain illegally. In addition, although Henry's statute of 1487 seemed to echo Edward's, Henry paid far greater attention to the actual interpretation of the law. The loophole over 'lawful' retaining was partly closed by interpreting it strictly and, although lawful retaining was allowed to continue, it was often accompanied by a recognisance to ensure the retinue was not misused. Henry took this further in the legislation of 1504. This act was harsher than his predecessor's because it omitted the ambiguous clause, and laid down much stricter methods of enforcement. It also introduced a novel system of licensing whereby men could employ retainers for the king's service alone. To do this a lord had to have a special licence endorsed with the privy seal, and the entire retinue had to be listed for royal approval. It was only valid during the king's lifetime.

1 Form of a licence to retain
Henry, by the grace of God, King of England and of France and Lord of
Ireland – greeting … we … by the advice of our Council, intending to
provide a good, substantial and competent number of captains and able
5 men of our subjects to be in readiness to serve us at our pleasure when
the case shall require, and trusting in your faith and truth, will and
desire you, and by these presents give unto your full power and authority from henceforth during our pleasure to take, appoint and retain
by indenture or covenant in form or manner as hereafter ensueth, and
10 none otherwise, such persons our subjects as by your discretion shall
be thought and seemeth to you to be able men to do us service in the
war in your company under you and at your leading at all times and
places and as often as it shall please us to command or asssign you, to
the number of persons, whose names be contained in a certificate by
15 you made in a bill of parchment indented betwixt us and you interchangeably signed by us and subscribed with your hand and to our secretary delivered … PROVIDED always that you retain not above the
said number which you shall indent for in form and manner hereafter
ensuing. PROVIDED also the same able persons shall not be chosen,
20 taken nor retained but only of your own tenants or of the inhabitants
within any office that you have of our grant …

d) How Successful was Henry in Curbing this Practice?

Evidence of Henry's success in this matter is seen in the reduction of
the numbers of retainers that magnates maintained. Those they had
appear to have been limited to the legitimate categories of servants,
officials and lawyers. However, studies of individual nobles, such as
the Duke of Buckingham or the Earl of Northumberland, show that
they might have got round official policy by employing more estate
officers than were necessary. Nor have any indentures (written con-
tracts of retaining) so far been discovered for Henry's reign similar to
those of the pre-1485 period, which suggests that the nobles must
have been very aware of the king's policy on retaining. If nobles did
retain without royal permission whilst Henry was on the throne, they
were careful not to leave any evidence. Examples were made of those
magnates who did break the law and were found out. In 1506 Lord
Abergavenny was fined the statutory £5 per month per retainer, which
amounted to the enormous sum of £70,550. Although Henry sus-
pended this in favour of a recognisance, the culprit had learned his
lesson and was an example to other would-be offenders. This was a
particularly extreme case, complicated because Abergavenny had also
been implicated in the Cornish rebellion. A more normal example
was that of the Earl of Devon who had given a recognisance not to
retain illegally in 1494 and then had to forfeit part of this for breaking his bond. The biggest difference in attitude between Edward IV
and Henry over retaining is seen in their reaction to their friends.

Whereas Edward turned a blind eye towards the misdemeanours of those close to him, Henry treated everyone alike. Among those indicted for illegal retaining in 1504 were the Duke of Buckingham, the Earls of Derby, Essex, Northumberland, Oxford and Shrewsbury, and even the king's mother, Lady Margaret, Countess of Richmond and Derby! One of the most celebrated victims of the king's displeasure over retaining was the Earl of Oxford, a friend and highly valued adviser. Francis Bacon gives an account of this in his history of Henry's reign, written in 1622:

1 There remaineth to this day a report that the king was on a time entertained by the Earl of Oxford, that was his principal servant for war and peace, nobly and sumptuously at his castle at Henningham. And at the king's going-away, the earl's servants stood in a seemly manner, in their
5 livery coats with cognisances, ranged on both sides, and made the king a lane. The king called the earl to him and said, 'My lord, I have heard much of your hospitality, but I see it is greater than the speech. These handsome gentlemen and yeomen, which I see on both sides of me, are sure your menial servants?' The earl smiled and said, 'It may please your
10 grace, that were not for mine ease. They are most of them my retainers, that are come to do me service at such a time as this, and chiefly to see your grace.' The king started a little, and said, 'By my faith, my lord, I thank you for my good cheer, but I may not endure to have my laws broken in my sight. My attorney must speak with you.' And it is
15 part of the report, that the earl compounded for no less than 15,000 marks (ie. £10,000).

Retaining continued well into the reign of Elizabeth I so Henry certainly did not eliminate the practice, but he controlled it to a far greater extent than his predecessors and prevented it from being a significant problem.

4 Local Government

> **KEY ISSUE** How did Henry extend the power of the crown into the localities?

a) The Effects of the Wars of the Roses on Local Government

The problem of restraining the individual nobles in the provinces leads to the more comprehensive issue of how law was upheld in the countryside as a whole. Here Henry also relied on the magnates to help him. Local government was carried out by a complex network of local officials, such as Sheriffs and Justices of the Peace, who were directly responsible to the king. He communicated with them through written orders known as writs, and their work was checked by

Judges and Commissioners at regular intervals. This arrangement worked relatively well under a strong king, who could ensure that his instructions were obeyed and that the local nobility did not develop too much power, or seize the opportunity to pursue their private feuds. However, during the Wars of the Roses the system had completely collapsed and Edward IV had had to attempt to rebuild this structure of local government almost from scratch. He had tried to do this in two ways. He travelled around the country intervening in disputes and personally hearing cases in the common law courts, and he appointed powerful local magnates to control particular areas. This system proved quite successful. One of the reasons for this was that Edward had delegated responsibility to only a small number of favoured nobles. But this had led to the creation of over-mighty subjects and had caused discontent among those who had felt overlooked. These over-mighty subjects were nobles who controlled vast areas of land throughout the country which gave them an enormous amount of power and influence. Generally Edward had been able to contain them but, on the sudden usurpation of Richard III, many seized their opportunity to take authority into their own hands and deliberately chose to ignore royal commands.

b) How far did Henry allow individual Magnates to build up Power in the Localities?

Henry saw the strengths in Edward's policy and followed it in principle, but, wherever possible, he stopped individuals building up too much power and he always insisted on their absolute loyalty to the Tudor dynasty. So, although the Stanley family was allowed to enhance its authority and to continue in charge of south Lancashire and Cheshire, control of the south-west of the country was taken away from the Marquess of Dorset after his treachery early in the reign. Two of Henry's strongest supporters were rewarded with estates which brought with them a considerable amount of local control: Jasper Tudor, Duke of Bedford, became the most influential nobleman in Wales, while the Earl of Oxford became powerful in East Anglia – although their influence never equalled that of Edward's leading nobles. Supporters of Richard III found it virtually impossible to regain the positions that they had enjoyed under the Yorkists. Although the Earl of Northumberland was allowed to continue in his former role of Lord Lieutenant of the North, his powers were greatly restricted and, on his death in 1489, Henry used the fact that the Percy heir was a minor to replace the Earl with Thomas Howard, Earl of Surrey, who had neither land nor influence in the northern counties. Surrey's judgements were therefore likely to be less partial. In addition, as Surrey was hoping to win back the lands and title lost by his father after Bosworth, Henry could expect good service from him. In 1501 the northern families were once again overlooked when

Surrey was replaced by a council under the Archbishop of York. The same pattern emerged in Wales after the deaths of Jasper Tudor (d.1495) and the Prince of Wales (d. 1502). Control was in the hands of a council under the presidency of William Smyth, Bishop of Coventry and Lichfield, who had no power base in the principality. So by the end of his reign Henry was moving away from the idea of appointing a local potentate to control a particular region. This prevented the growth of magnate power and over-mighty subjects in the provinces and in doing so forged far stronger links between central and local government.

c) How far did the King centralise Royal Power in the Provinces?

Supervision from the centre was the key feature of the exercise of law in the localities. However, this did not mean that Henry made royal progresses around the kingdom, involving himself in cases in a personal way, as Edward IV had done. Instead, he was the central figure directing all operations from London and making his commands felt in three ways: through the exploitation of crown lands, by encouraging more frequent use of the royal council and its offshoots for the settlement of local lawsuits, and by increasing the powers of the JPs. The first of these methods is fully discussed on pages 74–5, but it is clear that Henry's more efficient management and exploitation of all that the crown lands had to offer extended the authority of the monarch to all parts of the country, as well as increasing the income he received in rents. The second method is discussed in the section on central government (pages 58–9). In utilising the third method – developing the role of the JPs, who owed their offices to the king – Henry was also exerting his control more effectively over the localities.

d) The Role of the Justices of the Peace

Since the middle of the fourteenth century governments had given increased responsibility to the Justices of the Peace, who had gradually superseded the Sheriffs as the chief local government officers. JPs were responsible for the defence of public order and for implementing the various statutes of a social and economic nature, such as those concerned with the regulation of wages and the guilds. The JPs were appointed annually from among the local landowners. The average number commissioned for a county was about 18. The local bishop would usually head the list of those appointed, with the lay landowners following in strict order of social precedence. Although some of the largest landowners were sometimes chosen to be JPs, it was the knights and squires who carried out the majority of the commission's duties on a daily basis. But four times a year Quarter Sessions were held

On these occasions all the Justices had to attend so that they could try those accused of the more serious crimes – except treason, which was left to the council to investigate. Although JPs had the authority to pass judgement on all other crimes, more difficult cases were traditionally passed to the Assize Courts. The Assizes were sessions held twice a year in each county in England by professional judges acting under special commission from the crown. The position of JP did not carry with it any form of payment because it had always been felt that to offer rewards for such work would be inappropriate. This was because it was thought to be a natural part of the landowning classes' responsibility to ensure an effective system of law enforcement. As property owners, it was also in their own interest to do so.

After 1485 JPs continued to be selected from those with significant amounts of land. However, like Edward IV, Henry VII frequently chose to rely on the second rank of each county's landowners as it was another way of weakening the power of the greater magnates which had led to the corruption of justice at the local level so often in the past. He also followed the example of his predecessor in widening the scope of JPs' responsibilities. In 1461 Edward IV had transferred the criminal jurisdiction of the Sheriff to them. In 1485 an act of parliament gave them power to arrest and question poachers or hunters in disguise, because this could be a cover for murder or rebellion. Two years later they were given the power to grant bail to those awaiting trial. Further acts in 1495 dealt with the problem of corrupt or intimidated juries, which had often been used by men of influence as a way of escaping punishment. JPs were given the power to replace suspect members of juries, to act in cases of non-capital offences without a jury, and also to reward their informers. Of course, Henry had to rely on the Justices' own self-interest as leaders of society for the upholding of law and order. Virtually his only control over them was the threat of removal from the commission if they acted improperly. This would be regarded by most JPs as a considerable social disgrace.

However, JPs could only exercise their powers to a limited extent. Just as the king was dependent on them for the maintenance of law and order in the counties, so they were dependent on lesser officials in the countryside to bring offenders to them. By law every hundred (a subdivision of a county) had to provide itself with a High Constable and every parish with a Petty Constable. However, this was not easily done as people found such responsibility made them unpopular and there was no significant remuneration. Frequently JPs had to apply considerable pressure to fill these positions and, as a result, many petty crimes went unpunished.

The Court of the King's Bench could override decisions made at a Quarter Session and, after 1485, JPs were commanded to read out a proclamation at the beginning of each session emphasising that grievances against Justices could be taken to either an Assize Judge or to the king. But neither of these enactments seems to have been very effective. Therefore, although Henry had made provision for flaws in the system to be corrected, the new appeal system does not appear to have been widely used. The weakness in this type of local government was that the king was dependent on the goodwill of his officials; a system of paid servants, as existed in France, would have been more efficient. However, given the financial constraints on the English crown, the system worked relatively effectively by late medieval standards.

The most frequent problems of a local nature that the king had to face were the disputes between members of the nobility. Henry has been criticised because of the small number of cases involving nobles brought before the higher courts. Historians originally interpreted this as a lack of real determination to enforce the law strictly, but later research has shown that, while minor cases were dealt with through the formal process of law, those involving more important individuals were often settled informally to avoid the slow and cumbersome legal system. Many of the rolls of court that exist from the reign have 'case halted' written over them, followed by evidence of a recognisance paid to the king to clear up the matter once and for all. Henry seems to have preferred this method of exerting financial pressure on his mightier subjects to settle their disputes and thousands of such recognisances exist, particularly from later in the reign. Although the problem of keeping the peace had not been completely solved, Henry had gone a long way to extending his control of the situation by centralising the system of local government. To do this he had had to ensure that the organs of central government functioned efficiently.

5 Central Government

> **KEY ISSUES** How was central government organised during Henry's reign? How well did it function?

a) The King's Council

The centre of any medieval English government was the king himself and the men he chose to advise him, who sat on his council. Henry's council differed very little from those of the Yorkists. The largest social grouping on the council was the clerics, who accounted for about half of the total membership between 1485 and 1509. Amongst the most favoured of them were John Morton (Chancellor from 1487 and later made a Cardinal and Archbishop of Canterbury) and Richard Fox (the King's Secretary and Bishop of Winchester). There was also a substantial number of nobles, which seems to weaken the case of those commentators who have claimed that Henry sought to oust them from government. However, what was different about Henry's council was that he demanded real service from those who sat on it, so that what counted was not noble blood but how loyal and useful a councillor proved to be. Those nobles who served him well were amply rewarded. Among these was John de Vere, the Earl of Oxford, who had supported Henry since his days in exile; he was given the offices of Great Chamberlain and Lord Admiral. Jasper Tudor received the dukedom of Bedford and the control of Wales. Henry wisely did not wish to alienate the former Yorkists permanently, so, once they had paid in some way for their 'treachery', they were given opportunities to prove their loyalty to the new regime. The Earl of Lincoln was a member of the council until he joined the Simnel rebellion, whilst Thomas Howard, Earl of Surrey, became a councillor after his release from the Tower and was appointed Lord Treasurer of England in 1501.

Although Henry's council contained numerous representatives of the nobility, only his uncle, the Duke of Bedford, his friend, the Earl of Oxford, and his step-father, Lord Stanley, the Earl of Derby, were really close to the king. It was probably this fact that gave rise to his reputation for being anti-noble. He did not rely on a particular nobleman or family as Edward IV and Richard III had done. Instead, Henry's chief advisers and servants were drawn from the ranks of the lesser landowners and from the professional classes (especially lawyers) – men like Edward Poynings, Reginald Bray and Edmund Dudley. As the king was exploiting his lands through more efficient methods of estate management, he needed servants who understood auditing and property laws, and who had administrative skills. Real ability in these areas was what mattered to Henry, not social class. The king himself was usually present at council meetings so he was very aware of how much individual councillors contributed.

The functions of the council were to advise the king over matters of state, to administer law and order, and to act in a judicial capacity. During Henry's reign there was a total of 227 councillors, but there were not more than 150 at any one time, most of whom rarely attended meetings. When all the active members were present the council totalled about 40. The difficulty in controlling this led Henry to use smaller committees formed from within the council, as his Yorkist predecessors had done, but on a more regular basis. Richard III had established one to deal with legal cases involving those who could not afford the high costs of the normal system. This latter committee was resurrected in the second half of Henry's reign as the Court of Requests. One of the first committees to be set up by Henry, in 1487, was one to undertake responsibility for the implementation of the act of livery and maintenance. Another was the Court of General Surveyors which audited the revenues coming in from the crown lands and from those of which the king was feudal overlord. In the past it was mistakenly thought that in 1487 an act was passed which established a special 'Court of Star Chamber' to deal with the nobles. However, the only legislation passed in that year in this context was to set up a tribunal to prevent the intimidation of juries and to stop retaining. This tribunal seems to have gone out of use by 1509 and it had no connection with the later Court of Star Chamber. There were meetings in the 'Star Chamber' during Henry's reign, but this was a room in the Palace of Westminster with stars painted on the ceiling. Here the council met to consider judicial matters, but it was not a separate court in its own right. The most famous committee begun under Henry was the Council Learned in the Law.

b) The Council Learned in the Law

The Council Learned in the Law (normally referred to simply as the Council Learned) was a small and very professional body. Its name derived from the fact that most of its members had some sort of legal training or experience. This council came into being in 1495 to defend the king's position as a feudal landlord. Initially it began as an offshoot of the Duchy of Lancaster and the Chancellor of the Duchy was in charge of it. But it grew rapidly to embrace dealings in all the crown's lands and the rights that accompanied them. It was responsible for keeping up to date with the wardship, marriage and relief of all the king's tenants, and the collection of the feudal dues that were owed to him. Contemporaries criticised it because it operated without a jury, but this was true of all the conciliar committees. In fact, it was done deliberately because of the frequent charges of bribery brought against juries. Why the Council Learned was particularly hated was because of its connection with bonds and recognisances as it supervised the collection of these financial penalties. By the end of the reign it had become the most detested but the most important of all Henry's institutions of government involved in the maintenance of law and order.

c) The Role of Empson and Dudley

The Council Learned became increasingly feared after the promotion of Sir Richard Empson to the Chancellorship of the Duchy and the Presidency of the Council Learned in 1504. Under the joint leadership of Empson and his colleague, Edmund Dudley, royal rights were scrupulously enforced. Henry's use of bonds and recognisances has already been discussed (see pages 47–8); this disciplinary use of financial penalties was certainly an effective way of keeping the peace, but under the management of these two councillors the practice seems to have become much more widespread. As Henry was by this time more secure than ever before, the harsh enforcement of such penalties by Empson and Dudley, through this court, was bitterly resented. They are also thought to have manipulated the system by falsely claiming that people owed feudal dues, such as wardship, where no such obligation existed. In fact, Dudley later confessed that he had acted illegally for the king in more than 80 cases. So hated had the pair become that on the Henry's death they were toppled in a palace coup led by the king's other servants.

6 Regional Government.

KEY ISSUES What was a) the nature and b) the structure of regional government?

a) Provincial Councils

Both the Council of the North and the Council of Wales originated in Yorkist times. They continued to function throughout Henry VII's reign, supporting whoever the king chose to send as his representative in those areas that were too remote from London to be effectively controlled from there. Both of these institutions differed from the conciliar committees in having a clearly defined function dating from before Henry came to the throne. Yet they were closely linked to the main council, enjoying similar administrative and judicial power to enable the law to be enforced swiftly and efficiently, and, of course, they were ultimately subordinate to the king. Henry was unlike his predecessors in that he required his council in London to keep a close watch on the activities of the two provincial councils. Thus these were yet another example of how he extended the authority of central government into the provinces; by relying on trusted servants such as Jasper Tudor and the Earl of Surrey to enforce his will in the outlying areas Henry was ensuring that personal government was felt in every corner of his realm.

b) Wales

From the point of view of administration the 'Dominion of Wales' was, broadly speaking, divided between the five counties (six if Flintshire is included) of the Principality and the fifty or so semi-independent lordships and counties of the March. The Principality had been ruled since 1301 by the King's eldest son. It was acknowledged to be separate from England, in consequence of which its shires did not return members to parliament. The lordships of the March were relics of the piecemeal Norman/English conquest of Wales in the two centuries before 1282. Each lordship had its own judicial and administrative systems and officials so that the King's writ, as it was famously said, did not run in the March. Consequently Wales suffered administrative chaos and was plagued by disorder, particularly during the Wars of the Roses. With the freedom to raise troops for war, the Marcher lords were drawn into the dynastic conflict on the side of both Yorkists and Lancastrians. Until Edward IV established a Council to govern Wales in 1471, no attempt had been made either to weld together into a single system the counties and lordships of the Principality and March, or to abolish the privileges of the individual Marcher lords. Although Edward never succeeded in either respect, his Council had improved the situation in Wales by restraining 'the wild Welshmen and the evil disposed persons from their accustomed murders and outrages'. More importantly, his Council had set a precedent which Henry determined to follow.

Like Edward IV, Henry appreciated the need for administrative order. This is why he revived the Council in about 1493 (the exact date is not known) appointing his seven-year-old son Arthur as its nominal head as Prince of Wales. Although Henry's own experience pointed out to him the danger of an invasion of England through Wales, unlike Richard III, he did not have to worry too much about a possible threat to his position from the Welsh. His family links and Welsh connections, highlighted and celebrated by native poets and writers, ensured for him the support of the people. He rewarded their faith in him by trusting them to see to their own affairs, hence his policy of appointing Welshmen to key positions in Wales. His control of Wales was helped by the fact that by 1495, due in part to inheritance and purchase, and on account of death and forfeiture, scarcely half a dozen Marcher lordships remained in private hands. Henry, therefore, governed directly, and indirectly, a larger proportion of the total area of Wales than any king had done before.

c) Ireland

As king of England Henry was also lord of Ireland. However, the island was not ruled in a conciliar way. The king appointed a Lord Lieutenant (in 1485 it was Jasper Tudor). This was an honorary position. The actual work of governing Ireland was carried out by a Lord Deputy. Ireland presented a far more difficult problem to Henry than any of the other outlying areas of the kingdom. Only in the English Pale, a narrow band of territory about 50 miles long to the north of Dublin, was the king's authority really felt. In the rest of the island the effective rulers were the Irish chieftains, with family loyalties similar to the Scottish clans. Of these the Geraldine and Butler families were the most important. At the beginning of the reign the Geraldine family held the most important offices, those of Lord Deputy and Chancellor of Ireland. Henry's predecessors had found that it was easier to bestow these positions on the Irish leaders if they wanted to avoid conflict. Henry quickly learnt the danger that Ireland could pose when Simnel and Warbeck received considerable support there. In 1492, after the Earl of Kildare (the leader of the Geraldine family) had recognised Perkin Warbeck's claim to the throne, the king deprived him of his position as Lord Deputy and his brother of the

Great Seal. Only after they had sought the king's pardon in person was Henry willing to restore their titles.

In 1494, Henry set about reorganising Irish government. He created his infant son, Prince Henry, Lord Lieutenant, so as to echo the nominal headship exercised by his elder son in Wales, and appointed Sir Edward Poynings, one of his most trusted advisers, as Deputy. Other appointments were also English to emphasise Henry's desire for obedience to England. Poynings' main task was to bring Ulster, the most rebellious area, under the king's control and to impose a constitution on Ireland that would ensure its future obedience to the English crown. However, he failed in Ulster, only succeeding in buying off the clans in return for a temporary promise of peace. He was more successful in the establishment of a constitution at the parliament which met at Drogheda in 1494; Poynings' Law, as it became known, decreed that an Irish parliament could only be summoned and pass laws with the king's prior approval. No future legislation was to be discussed unless it had first been agreed by the king and his council. In addition, any law made in England would automatically apply to Ireland. This gave the king far greater control over Ireland by destroying the independent legislative power of the Irish parliament. In the short term, he hoped to prevent the calling of an unauthorised Irish parliament, which might recognise another pretender. In the long term, it proved to be largely a theoretical victory. The expense of attempting to rule Ireland directly soon proved to be unsustainably high, and the experiment was abandoned. Henry returned to his earlier policy of ruling through the Irish chieftains. He is reported to have responded to the comment that all England could not rule Kildare, that Kildare had therefore better rule all Ireland! Kildare was reinstated as Lord Deputy and, for much of the rest of the reign, Ireland ceased to be a problem for Henry.

7 Parliament

> **KEY ISSUES** What part did parliament play in medieval government? What use did Henry make of it?

a) Background

In the fifteenth century, the government of England was clearly the responsibility of the king and his council. Parliament played no regular part in the maintenance of law and order. It met only to grant taxes and to pass laws, and it was in this latter role that it was of use to the king in the control he exerted over his subjects. Parliament was the meeting of the two Houses of Lords and Commons. The predominance of the Lords can be gauged by where they met – the Lords in a room in the royal palace of Westminster, and the Commons in the nearby chapter house of Westminster Abbey! The House of Lords was made up of two groups: the Lords spiritual (the archbishops, bishops and the heads of the more important monasteries) and the Lords temporal (the peers). Tradition gave the Lords greater authority than the Commons, and it was still the practice in 1485 for important legislation to be introduced first into the House of Lords. However, this was beginning to change before the end of the reign. The Commons was composed of MPs chosen by a very limited electorate made up of those who possessed considerable property. Two members were elected to represent each county and borough (a town with a royal charter granting privileges for services rendered, usually dating well back into the middle ages). The type of men typically sitting in the lower house were the local gentry representing the counties, and merchants and lawyers representing the boroughs. In practice parliament was the meeting of the king, his councillors and the Lords. The Commons met whilst the king discussed issues with the Lords, but he only spoke to them about particularly important issues, such as his right to the throne! They communicated with him through the Speaker, elected from amongst their number, but in fact a royal nominee. Parliament was only summoned when there was a special need to do so, and its meetings normally lasted only a few weeks.

b) Parliament in Henry VII's Reign

The fact that parliament met infrequently is evidence of its limited role in Henry's government. In the 24 years of his reign it met on only seven occasions, and five of those were in his first decade as king when he was relatively insecure in his possession of the throne. There were several reasons for this infrequency of meetings. Henry did not need to ask for war taxes very often because his foreign policy was based on avoiding expensive campaigns abroad. Nor did he wish to strain the loyalty of his subjects by too many requests for grants of money, so he found other ways of filling his treasury. Parliament's judicial function as the final court of appeal was now being fulfilled by the subsidiary courts of the Royal Council, such as the Council Learned in the Law. Finally, although Henry used parliament for introducing government bills, he did not feel the need to initiate legislation on a large scale. The type of acts most frequently passed were acts of attainder against the king's political opponents. So, from Henry's point of view, parliament was of particular use in helping him subdue his intractable magnates.

The king might not have summoned parliament frequently but, by the way he used it, he continued its traditional role as an institution where the most important business of the kingdom was transacted. This is clear not only in the number of attainders against individual nobles that he requested parliament to pass, but in the way he used it to ratify his claim to the throne in 1486. Legislation was also used to carry out his policies against riots and retaining, and 10 per cent of all statutes dealt with the responsibilities of the JPs and the control of the provinces. Further acts dealt with social discipline, such as that of 1495 which laid down maximum wages and minimum hours of work. Another act ordered that vagabonds should be put in the stocks and returned to their original place of residence. Perhaps most importantly, the act of 1504, which forbade corporations from making any regulations unless they first had the approval of the king, showed the way in which parliament was being used, to emphasise the fact that all power derived from the crown and that there was only one ruler in England. So, although parliament did not meet on a regular basis during Henry's reign, there was no threat of it ceasing to exist as a political institution. The king used it as and when circumstances demanded, just as his predecessors had done.

8 Conclusion: Henry establishes good Government and restores Law and Order

> **KEY ISSUE** How far did Henry establish good governance and restore law and order?

Henry largely achieved his ambition of restoring law and order – although by late medieval standards, rather than by those of the present day. However, his way of doing this was different from that of his predecessors. His style of rule was one of personal government; Henry ruled as the master of the most important household in the kingdom (in the next chapter we shall examine his innovative use of the Privy Chamber). He accomplished this by increasing the authority of the monarchy and by striving to ensure that all his subjects, rich and poor alike, respected and obeyed his will. He immediately recognised the potential threat posed by the nobility, aware of the way in which they had seized the opportunity to assert their authority under a weak king. He largely succeeded in preventing them from manipulating the law to suit their own purposes by insisting on absolute loyalty from those who gained his confidence and carried out his commands. However, he did not oust them from government, as used to be thought. He was happy to work closely with those nobles he judged to be worthy of his trust, and the practice of entrusting control of the outlying areas of the country to the magnates continued, as, for example, with the Earl of Surrey in the north. But, far more than his predecessors, he strictly enforced the laws against livery and maintenance, ensuring that all obeyed and that no tempting loopholes remained. As a result of his policies, he faced few challenges from over-mighty subjects, and by deliberately refraining from creating many new peers, his magnates became a small, select and loyal group, with those daring to disobey him facing crippling financial penalties.

To Henry, personal monarchy meant supervision from the centre and the delegation of authority in the localities only to those who could be trusted. Power was not given to people merely because of their exalted parentage. Henry built up the power of the JP as the most important local official and, in so doing, placed power in the hands of the gentry who, as lesser landowners, were less able to resist the king's will than were their more powerful neighbours. The council became more efficient under Henry's painstaking administration and the responsibilities of its various committees were carefully defined so as to ensure that the king's orders were carried out in all parts of the country. Of course, there were still problems. Poor communications and the geography of the kingdom often hindered the speedy transmission of the king's instructions. Henry remained reliant on those to whom he delegated his powers, for there was no body of men responsible directly to him. England still did not have a formal police like the Hermandad in Spain, or a standing army. However, compared to the state of the country when he came to the throne, England was relatively law-abiding by the time he died. Strong leadership, increased centralisation and the often careful delegation of offices meant that English society was once again generally at peace with itself.

Summary Diagram

Good Governance

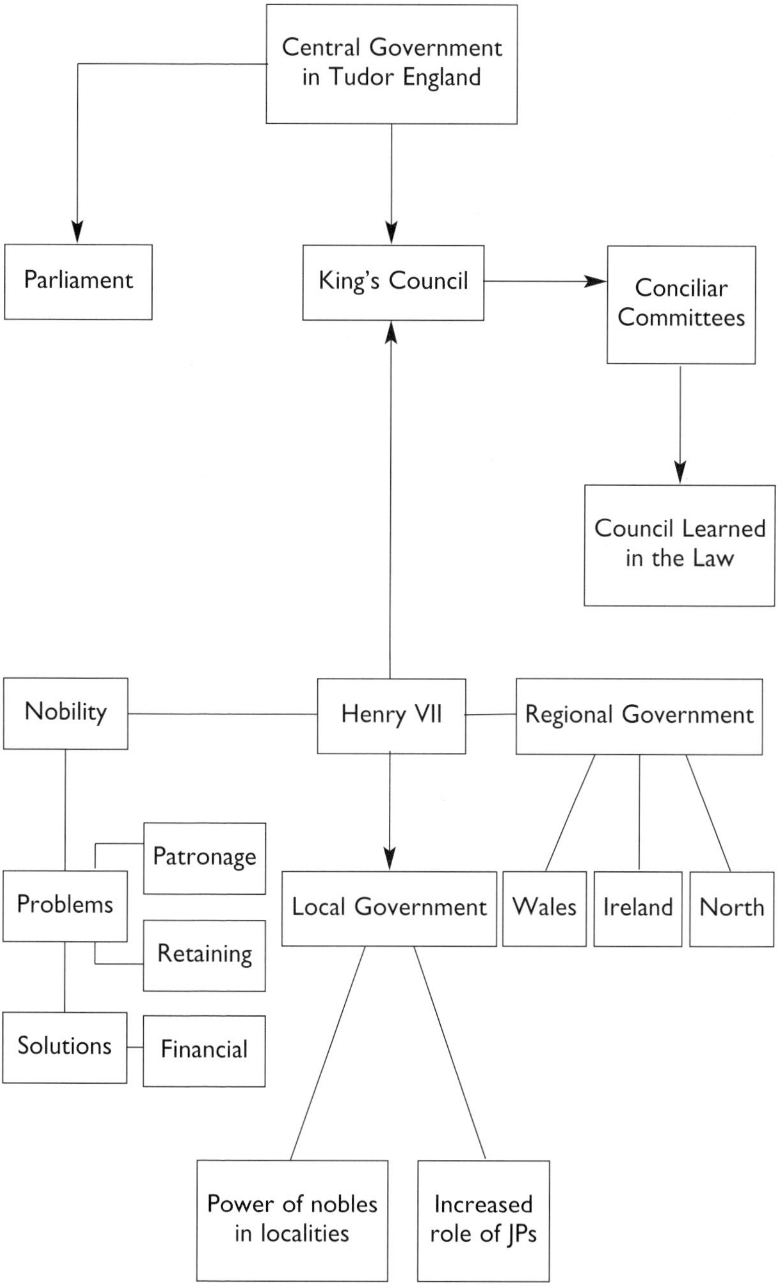

Working on Chapter 3

You need to make outline notes on how Henry established good governance but do select some examples as well of his more general methods. Great detail is not required, as complex factual knowledge is not usually needed for this topic. Nevertheless, you should acquaint yourself with the key issues and be prepared to furnish each with an easy to read, and understand, written answer. This can be done in the form of bullet points, some of which are provided in the summary diagram. Do make notes about the problems Henry faced and the methods he used to overcome them. Compare the policies Henry and his Yorkist predecessors pursued and highlight those areas where he introduced his own ideas. This is a topic which easily lends itself to discussion and/or debate. The following issues might be considered suitable motions for debate where a case can be made for and against, and argued before your classmates.

1. Henry deliberately tried to oust the nobility from their traditionally advisory role to the crown.
2. The king's ruthless financial exploitation of the nobility is evidence of his rapaciousness.
3. Henry's use of parliament shows it had but a marginal role in medieval government.

Answering structured and essay questions on Chapter 3

Since this topic has been the subject of serious revision by historians, particularly Henry's relationship with the nobility, you can expect structured questions to be set on aspects of his government.

If the paper you are sitting is made up of four-part structured questions you might find that they are worded as follows:

a) Identify four steps taken by Henry VII to strengthen his position as king in the early years of his reign. *(4 marks)*
b) Explain briefly how Henry VII attempted to curb retaining. *(5 marks)*
c) To what extent did Henry VII succeed in promoting the enforcement of law and order in the localities? *(7 marks)*
d) Was there any significant innovation in the government of Henry VII? Explain your answer fully. *(9 marks)*

Remember to identify the key words before you begin planning your answers.

In (a) and (b) the examiner is seeking to test your historical knowledge and understanding. Therefore you should keep your answers

brief and to the point, especially for (a) which requires only bullet point responses.

In (c) and (d) the examiner is testing your ability to analyse and evaluate, therefore it is important to remember that marks will be awarded both for the factual content of your answer and for the analytical skills you display.

The answers to each of the above questions can easily be found in the chapter. You will need to consult chapter 4 in order to answer (d) fully.

Essay questions are rarely set on this topic alone. However, this does not mean that it is not important! The way Henry VII restored law and order is a major part of most general questions on his reign. These will be dealt with in the concluding chapter. Occasionally such a question as this might appear:

1. By what means and with what success did Henry VII re-establish the primacy of the monarchy over the great magnates?

This is a common way of phrasing a question at this level. The key words are 'by what means', 'with what success' – meaning how did Henry try to subdue the nobles and ensure their loyalty, and how successful was he? – and 're-establish' – which suggests that something had been lost, possibly by his predecessors. Draw up a plan listing Henry's policies towards the nobles and make a note of how successful each was in practice. The most effective way of doing this is to have a pen and paper with you as you re-read this chapter. Concentrate your reading on sections 2 and 3, divide your paper in half and list your points on one side with a comment on their success or failure on the other side. Then arrange them in order, either starting with his least successful and ending with the most successful or the other way round.

Source-based questions on Chapter 3

1. The Theory of Obligation

Read the extracts from *A Mirror for Magistrates*, edited by William Baldwin, and from Sir John Fortescue on page 41. Answer the following questions:

a) According to Baldwin why was it justifiable for a traitor to come to a 'fearful end'? *(2 marks)*

b) In what way does Fortescue stress the need for an established hierarchy? *(3 marks)*

c) Compare the content of the two extracts. What similarities can you detect in their philosophies of life? *(4 marks)*

d) From your reading of Chapters 2 and 3, how far were the ideas

expressed in these extracts put into practice during the reign of Henry VII? Consider the rebellions he faced and his attitude towards the nobility. *(6 marks)*

2. *Retaining*

Read the Indenture of Retainder issued by Edward IV in 1481 (pages 49–50), the Licence to Retain issued by Henry VII (page 51), and the extract from Francis Bacon's *History of the Reign of King Henry the Seventh* (page 52). Answer the following questions:

a) What is meant by 'saving the allegiance which the same Ralph oweth to the king our sovereign lord and to the prince'? (page 50, line 11) *(2 marks)*

b) Why did Henry try to curb retaining by legislation and yet at the same time issue special licences endorsing it? *(3 marks)*

c) How does Henry's licence differ from Edward's indenture in the privileges it gives? *(4 marks)*

d) Using all three documents, what do we learn about the way in which Henry VII's attitude towards retaining differed from that of Edward IV? *(5 marks)*

e) Why did Henry VII consider it to be so important to control the nature and extent of retaining and maintenance? *(6 marks)*

With sets of questions such as the above, make sure that you note well the number of marks that have been allocated for each part. Almost without exception, you should plan the amount of time you spend on each part directly in proportion to the marks awarded for it.

4 Financial Policy

POINTS TO CONSIDER

This chapter is designed to show i) what the crown's financial resources were when Henry VII came to the throne, ii) the areas in which he made substantial changes, and iii) the extent to which he increased the annual revenue of the crown by the end of his reign.

When reading the chapter for the first time you should bear in mind the accusations made of Henry down the centuries, that he unfairly exploited his sources of revenue to make the crown rich at the expense of his subjects. You also need to assess the validity of these criticisms.

KEY DATES

1485 Sir Thomas Lovell appointed Treasurer of the Chamber, becoming the chief financial officer of the crown.

1487 First of four ('90, '91, '97 were the other three) parliaments convened to raise traditional taxes of fifteenths and tenths.

1487 Henry began the restoration of the Chamber to its former position at the head of the crown's financial administration.

1492 By the terms of the Treaty of Étaples, France agreed to pay Henry £159,000 in instalments of £5,000; Sir John Heron appointed to replace Lovell.

1503 Office of the Master of Wards established.

1 Introduction

> **KEY ISSUE** What has been the traditional assessment of Henry's financial prowess?

References to Henry's financial prowess abound. He has been credited with being 'the best business man ever to sit upon the English throne', and on his death he was described as the 'richest lord that is now known in the world'. These opinions are exaggerated: he died solvent, but that was all. However, both his contemporaries and later historians have concentrated on emphasising his financial success. In spite of his lack of experience in government, Henry was acutely aware of the importance of strong finances if he was to remain safely on his throne. The recent uncertainty of the succession, culminating in his own usurpation of the crown, meant there was always the possibility of others putting forward their own claim. Financial stability was essential if he was to be able to fund enough soldiers to defeat them.

In addition, if the succession was still challenged at the time of his death, a full treasury would provide his son with the resources to fight to retain his throne.

Ever since the seventeenth century, when Francis Bacon wrote with awe of Henry's success in improving the financial position of the crown, Henry's reputation as a ruler has largely rested on his assumed financial acumen. From this have arisen the criticisms that Henry was avaricious and that by the end of his reign he was bleeding every available source of income to its limits. More recently historians have questioned Henry's ingenuity in this sphere of administration. They have claimed that his methods of raising money were not new, but that he was simply following the example of his Yorkist predecessors. So, when examining his financial policy, there are three questions that must be answered: 'How rapacious was Henry?', 'How innovative were the methods he used to increase the revenues of the crown?', and 'How successful was he in his financial policy?'.

One of the constraints facing Henry in the management of his financial affairs was that throughout the middle ages English kings were expected to 'live of their own'. It was even a part of their coronation oath that they would do so. This meant that they had to manage on the regular income that came to them annually in their capacities as monarchs and landowners. The king could not ask parliament for a grant (additional taxation) except in unusual circumstances, such as war. There was always the fear that, if additional direct taxes were demanded frequently, rebellion might soon follow.

2 Financial Administration

> **KEY ISSUES** What was the nature of medieval financial institutions? On whom did the king rely to run them?

a) Financial Institutions: The Exchequer and the Chamber

Since the twelfth century the centre of the crown's financial administration had been the Exchequer. This had two functions: to receive, store and pay out money, and to audit the accounts. To organise this department and prevent fraud and embezzlement there was a complex hierarchy of officials. Although it worked in a relatively honest and reliable fashion for the time, it did have flaws. The system was infuriatingly slow and cumbersome. Outstanding sums often took years to collect, and audits were equally behind time. It was because of this that the Yorkist kings had developed the Chamber as their financial department. This was a more informal and flexible system, partly because it had not been involved in royal finance for very long. It had originated from the accounting system used on the estates of the great nobles, who appointed officials called receivers and auditors from within their household to run certain groups of their estates, particularly in their absence. Edward IV had been familiar with this practice on the Yorkist estates, so when he became king he had applied it to the royal estates. He had chosen to use the King's Chamber, the innermost part of the king's household, to handle his finances in an attempt to exert more personal control over what happened. Henry VII had neither the experience nor the time to continue this practice initially – a decision which he must later have regretted – so the Exchequer resumed its control of royal finances. However, as early as 1487 Henry admitted that in focusing so intensely on his own security, he had neglected to take adequate care of his estates and that they had 'greatly fallen into decay'. The accounts bear witness to this. In Richard III's reign they had brought in £25,000 per annum, but by 1486 this had declined to £12,000.

In 1487 Henry began to restore the Chamber system to its former position as the most important institution of financial administration. By the late 1490s it was once again the centre of royal finance, handling an annual turnover well in excess of £100,000. It dealt with the transfer of all revenue from crown lands, profits of justice, feudal dues, and the French pension – in fact, all sources of income except custom duties and the accounts of the Sheriffs (the officials responsible for the maintenance of law and order in the shires). These remained under the control of the Exchequer because their collection involved detailed information and a complex organisation of officers and records not available to the Treasurer of the Chamber. Richard III had laid the basis for the reform of the financial administration and Henry was able to continue this with the help of his officials, many of whom had been trained under the Yorkist regime.

The development of the Chamber into the national treasury automatically led to further reorganisation within the household, from where the Chamber had originated. The department that increased most in importance was the king's 'Privy Chamber', made up of his personal household servants. This now took over the administration of the royal household as well as taking care of Henry's private expenditure, formerly a responsibility of the Chamber. The chief officer of the Privy Chamber, the Groom of the Stool, became second in preeminence to the Treasurer of the Chamber. In addition, lesser household officials, such as Gentlemen of the Bedchamber, grooms and ushers, found that new opportunities for promotion were open to them. The transformation of the Privy Chamber is important because it continued to play a vital role in Tudor government throughout the sixteenth century, and many Tudor ministers rose from its ranks.

The theoretical head of the financial system was the Treasurer of England, but he had long been merely a figurehead and the office was traditionally bestowed on an important noble as an honorary position. In practice, the Treasurer of the Chamber had become the chief financial officer of the crown. Under Henry VII, this position was held by two of the king's most stalwart and efficient servants, Sir Thomas Lovell (1485–92), and Sir John Heron (1492–1521). The main advantage of the Chamber system to the king was that it gave him much closer control over his finances; and what gave it even greater impetus was that Henry worked alongside both men, checking the accounts himself and leaving his signature as proof at the end of each page. The two entries illustrated below show where he began to write his initial in a different and possibly quicker way.

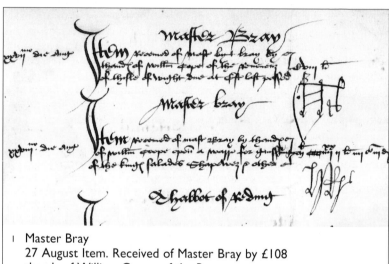

  1 Master Bray
      27 August Item. Received of Master Bray by £108
      thands of William Coope of the Reveneuz
      of thisle of Wight due at Ester last
  5 passed

      Master Bray
      28 August Item. Received of Master Bray by £1,382 4s.3d.
      thands of William Coope upon a war-
      rant for garnisshing of the king's
 10 salades, shapewex and other

Chamber Receipts, August 1492

b) Financial Personnel

The personal nature of this revived financial administration demanded loyalty, efficiency and integrity from the officials in charge, and Henry both chose carefully and was well served. His most trusted adviser in financial matters was his friend, Sir Reginald Bray, the Chancellor of the Duchy of Lancaster. Bray had come to Henry's attention as an important member of his mother's household. He sat in parliament and was a valued councillor, but it was as Chancellor of the Duchy of Lancaster, in charge of administering one of the richest, most efficient and, therefore, most important groups of royal estates in the country, that Henry became aware of his administrative skills. His power did not depend on his official position. It depended on the fact that he held the trust and confidence of the king – thus illustrating once again the personal role of the monarch in government. Bray had been responsible for successfully restoring the effective methods of estate management at the Duchy which had been thrown into turmoil by the civil disorder of the 1450s and by Richard III's usurpation of power. It was for this reason that Henry entrusted him with the position of Treasurer of the Chamber and the task of introducing new methods of auditing the accounts. Bray did not work in isolation. He co-operated closely with Heron and other household officials, making the system more efficient by holding frequent meetings to discuss and examine the Chamber accounts.

3 The Financial Resources of the Crown

> **KEY ISSUE** What is meant by ordinary and extraordinary revenue?

Historians frequently make a distinction between two separate types of revenue that rulers received at this time. These are the 'ordinary' revenue which came in every year, although in fluctuating amounts, and the 'extraordinary' revenue, usually in the form of a parliamentary grant, which the king had to request from his subjects, usually in an emergency. It is important to clarify what is meant by both these terms because they are so frequently used, and it is a useful distinction to make because it helps us to distinguish between the revenues which the king controlled himself and those which were dependent on the consent of others. Ordinary revenue came from crown lands and custom duties, but also included the profits of justice and feudal taxes on lands held in return for military service. Extraordinary revenue derived from the subject's obligation to help the king in time of need and by the fifteenth century this usually meant taxation levied in parliament. Less frequently it could also be money which came to the king as feudal overlord, a right which belonged to any feudal lord; this was known as a 'feudal aid' and was levied on specific occasions. For example, if the king was captured and held to ransom, he could demand an aid to raise the money necessary to obtain his release. It could also be money raised by borrowing from his richer subjects in an emergency, or gifts from other rulers, often granted as part of a favourable peace treaty.

4 Ordinary Revenue

> **KEY ISSUES** What different forms of ordinary revenue were
> available to Henry? How successfully did he exploit them?

a) Crown Lands

The most important way in which Henry increased his ordinary revenue was by maximising the yield from crown lands. This was partly
due to greater efficiency in their administration, but was mainly
because, unlike Edward IV, he did not grant a large proportion of
them to his family and supporters, and thus retained all the profits
from them for himself. Coming to the throne at the end of the Wars
of the Roses, he inherited all the lands which had belonged to the
houses of York and Lancaster, including the Earldoms of Richmond,
March and Warwick, the Duchy of Lancaster and the Principality of
Wales. On the deaths of his mother and his wife, their lands came to
him as well. He also further enriched the crown through escheats –
where men died without heirs, their lands passed by right to the king
– and by attainders, a frequent method of punishment used by the
king which resulted in the profits from the attainted person's estates
coming to the crown. Henry recognised the importance of land from
the start, encouraging his first parliament of 1486 to pass the Act of
Resumption which recovered for the crown all properties granted
away since 1455. However, having stated his claim, he did not take
back all the estates involved.

The Duchy of Lancaster, which had come to the crown with Henry
IV in 1399, played a key role in transforming and updating the administration of the rest of the crown lands, and is a good example of how
Henry VII capitalised on this source of income to the full. Unlike
other groups of crown lands, the Duchy had its own organisation centred around its Chancellor and it had adopted the new methods of
estate management long before most noblemen or the king. At the
beginning of Henry's reign it brought in £650 per year to the
Chamber, but by 1509 this had increased tenfold under the skilful
and more stringent management of Sir Reginald Bray. Edward IV
had introduced similar methods of estate administration to the rest
of the crown lands, which had increased the revenue from them, but
Henry demanded even greater efficiency. The accounts were rigor-
ously checked by the king and the receivers, and the chief financial
officers for the individual estates were encouraged to make ever
bigger profits.

Henry also pursued a policy towards his lands that was different
from that of Edward IV. This was partly due to his personal circumstances. He was lucky in having few relatives who expected to benefit
from his territorial acquisitions. There were no brothers; his uncle,

Jasper Tudor, died in 1495, and his elder son, Arthur, in 1502. This left only Prince Henry requiring provision. Henry VII had no obvious favourites, nor was he inclined to shower honours on his supporters. Therefore on his death the crown lands were more extensive than they had ever been. Efficient management, a thrifty nature and good fortune meant that the annual income from crown lands had increased from £29,000 on the death of Richard III in 1485 to £42,000 in 1509.

b) Customs Duties

At the beginning of Henry's reign customs duties made up the largest part of the king's income, but by 1509 they had been overtaken by the revenue from crown lands. However, they were still providing a third of the ordinary revenue. In the late fifteenth century the principal duties levied were on wool, leather, cloth and wine, but the rate at which many of these (such as the duties on cloth) were levied had not changed since 1347. Under Edward the average yearly yield had increased due to his encouragement of trade and a tighter administration, which cut down on embezzlement at all levels. Henry followed his example successfully by blocking many of the loopholes in the system. For example, from 1487 merchants involved in coastal trading, shipping merchandise from one English port to another, were required to produce a certificate from the first port specifying the transaction and the duties paid. In 1496 he tried to reduce some of the privileges gained by foreign merchants in the past. Twice during his reign he updated the Book of Rates of customs duties to be paid in London. The ways in which he encouraged trade are discussed on pages 95–102. However, despite Henry's efforts, income from customs did not greatly increase. The average annual receipts were about £33,000 for the first 10 years of the reign and about £40,000 thereafter. Smuggling seems to have continued, in spite of stricter control, and even Henry could not manipulate international trade entirely to his whim: it was dependent on the fragile and fluctuating relationships of all the European powers.

c) Feudal Dues

Another part of the crown's income were the feudal dues, paid by those who held land from the king in return for military service. This was an outdated remnant of the feudal system that had not yet withered away. As the greatest feudal lord, the king was owed certain obligations by his tenants-in-chief (those holding their land directly from the crown), just as they in turn were owed the same duties by their tenants. These included wardship, whereby the king took control of the estates of minors (those who were too young to be legally responsible for their inheritance) in the capacity of their guardian until they came of age, and received most of the profits from their estates. Feudal dues also included marriage (the royal right to give unmarried heirs and heiresses in marriage at a profit to the crown), livery (the payment made to recover lands out of wardship), and the fine known as 'relief' which the king received on the transfer of lands through inheritance. Henry was determined to enforce these traditional rights to the full and to extract the maximum income possible from them. Initially the proceeds from wardship and marriage were small, amounting to only £350 in 1487, but after 1503 a special officer (the Master of the King's Wards) was appointed to supervise them, and by 1507 the annual income had risen to £6,000.

d) Profits of Justice

As monarch, Henry was head of the judicial system and was therefore entitled to its profits. The law courts yielded income in two ways: the fees paid for the legal writ or summons to court, necessary for any case to begin, and the fines levied by the courts as punishment. The former provided a continuous and not inconsiderable income, but the amount raised by the latter was much larger. After Henry's death it was widely claimed that he had perverted the legal system by charging his leading subjects with technical crimes merely in order to profit from the fines that could then be imposed on them. It appears that these allegations were unfounded. Certainly, legal fines made a significant contribution to Henry's income but, although high, they were exacted mainly for serious crimes. There is no evidence to suggest that most of the culprits were anything other than guilty of the offences with which they were charged. However, he did ensure that most criminal acts, including treason, were punished by fines rather than by imprisonment or execution. This yielded him much more profit, as happened with his treatment of the rebels after the insurrection in Cornwall in 1497. Even in lesser cases, Henry appears to have put financial gain first and, although he did not resort to reviving obsolete laws just in order to profit from them, he did exploit the system. The number of receipts from sales of pardons for murder and other cases that still survive are evidence of this. The example of the Earl of Northumberland, who was ordered to pay £10,000 for ravishing a royal ward, was probably a way of compensating the income that Henry had lost with the ending of the earl's minority! Another type of fine that the king used as punishment against opponents was that of attainder. Sir William Stanley brought the crown £9,000 in cash (in income from his lands) and £1,000 per annum in this way after his treason in 1495. There was only one parliament during the reign which omitted to pass any attainders and the highest number in any session was 51.

5 Extraordinary Revenue

> **KEY ISSUES** What different forms of extraordinary revenue were
> available to Henry? How successfully did he exploit them?

a) Parliamentary Grants

Extraordinary revenue was money which came to the crown on particular occasions and therefore with no regularity. It arose from the
obligation of the king's subjects to help him when the national
interest was threatened. By the later middle ages the principal form
of such assistance was a sum of money granted by parliament.
Henry did not misuse this right. Like his Tudor descendants, he
was reluctant to tax unless absolutely necessary, as he was wary of
being forced to surrender freedom of action in exchange for
money. During the fifteenth century the Lancastrian kings had
encountered difficulties with parliament as it realised its bargaining
position, demanding restrictions on the king's power in exchange
for grants of money. Henry was therefore cautious in his demands
for money from parliament. However, he did request financial
assistance in 1487 to pay for the Battle of Stoke, in 1489 to go to
war against the French, and in 1496 to defend the throne against
the attack from the Scots and Perkin Warbeck. Historians have
accused Henry of cheating his subjects by raising money for wars
that never actually took place, as in 1496. Certainly, Henry received
the grant from parliament after the initial invasion of the Scots had
failed to cross the border, but it could be argued that the money
was still needed as the attack might have been renewed at any time.
In the event, there was no further trouble from the northern kingdom, but some of the money was used to suppress a rebellion in
Cornwall.

The usual type of tax levied was a national assessment, a fifteenth
and tenth, on a subject's movable goods – a fifteenth in the countryside and a tenth in the towns. Several of these grants could be levied
by one parliament, depending how much the king needed. This was
not really satisfactory as it was based on town and county assessments
that were centuries out of date, and which therefore did not tap anything approaching all the available taxable wealth of the country. So
in 1489, when he needed £100,000 to finance the French war, Henry
tried another method – a form of income tax, a practice tried only
twice before. However, the innovation was largely a failure as only
about a third of the anticipated amount was actually collected. As a
result, in 1496 Henry returned to the established method of taxation,
and it was left to his successors to develop more efficient systems of
direct taxation.

b) Loans and Benevolences

The king could also rely on loans from his richer subjects in times of emergency. In 1496 Henry was desperate for extra cash to defeat Warbeck and the Scots. He appealed to his people:

> This is a thing of so great weight and importance as may not be failed, and therefore fail ye not thereof for your said part ... as ye intend the good and honour of us and of this our realm; and as ye tender also the weal and surety of yourself.

Such requests were obviously virtually impossible for people to decline, even though they were traditionally in the form of 'agreements' between the two parties. Henry seems to have asked for only modest sums and there is no evidence of any resentment, probably as most of the loans appear to have been repaid. He probably had little choice but to repay them, with pretenders to the throne at large for the greater part of the reign! Subjects with a grievance because they were owed money by the king were more likely to support a rival claimant to the throne.

Rather a different matter was the benevolence – a type of forced loan with which there was no question of repayment. This had been introduced by Edward IV in 1475 when he was preparing to invade France. It was a general tax more far-reaching than the fifteenth and tenth. Subjects were asked to contribute to the king's expenses as a sign of their good will towards him at a time of crisis and, if not resorted to often, it was an effective way of raising money. In 1491 Henry raised a forced loan when he intended to take his army across the Channel; this produced £48,500, a considerable amount when compared with the sums yielded by direct taxation. Royal Commissioners were stringent in its collection. One lady offering only £5 of the £20 deemed appropriate for her to contribute was threatened with being summoned before the king's council. This is what Polydore Vergil wrote in his *Anglica Historia* about the benevolence of 1491:

> 1 Accordingly, having summoned a council of his nobles, Henry asked them to decide to provide for this war with both men and money. All unanimously concurred in the reasons for war and offered their own best services. Having praised their martial resolution, the king – lest the
> 5 poor sort should be burdened with the charge of paying the troops for the war – levied money from the rich only, each contributing to the pay of the troops according to his means. Since it was the responsibility of each individual to contribute a great or a small sum, this type of tax was called a 'benevolence'; Henry in this copied King Edward IV, who first
> 10 raised money from the people under the name of loving kindness. In this process it could be perceived precisely how much each person cherished the king ... for the man who paid most was presumed to be most dutiful; many none the less secretly grudged their contribution, so that this method of taxation might more appropriately be termed a
> 15 'malevolence' rather than a 'benevolence'.

The *Great Chronicle of London* recorded the following in 1491:

1 The King ... sent for the Mayor [of London] and so handled him, that
   he caused him to grant towards his good speed, if his grace went in his
   proper person, £200. By precedent whereof all the aldermen were fain
   to do the same ... This benevolence was so chargeable unto the City
5 that the whole sum thereof extended unto £9,682 17s. 4d. By reason
   whereof it was named later malevolence for benevolence. Then the
   King visited many counties, and the commissioners the residue, and in
   such wise exhorted them that the King's grace was well contented with
   the loving demeanour of his subjects. And so he had good cause, for by
10 this way he levied more money than he should have done with four fifteenths, and also with less grudge of his commons, for to this charge
   paid none but men of good substance, whereas at every fifteenth are
   charged poor people, which makes more grudging for paying of six-
   pence than at this time many did for paying of six nobles.

c) Clerical Taxes

Henry received quite substantial sums from the Church, although
smaller amounts than later monarchs collected after the
Reformation, when the Church came under the control of the state.
On several occasions, usually when parliament made a grant, the
convocations (meetings of representatives of the clergy of the
Archdioceses of Canterbury and York) followed suit with their own
contributions. In 1489 they voted £25,000 towards the cost of the
French war. Henry was not averse to dabbling in the Renaissance vice
of simony (the selling of church appointments), charging £300 for
the Archdeaconry of Buckingham on one occasion. Like many of his
predecessors, the king practised the policy of keeping bishoprics
vacant for some time before making new appointments so that he
could pocket the revenue in the meantime. Due to a rash of deaths
amongst the bishops in the last years of the reign, Henry received over
£6,000 per annum in this way. However, he did not exploit this
method as much as some of his contemporaries in other countries;
whereas they often prolonged vacancies for years, he rarely left a
diocese without a bishop for more than 12 months.

d) Feudal Obligations

Another type of extraordinary revenue was connected with feudal
obligations. As the chief feudal lord, the king had the right to
demand feudal aid on special occasions, such as the knighting of his
eldest son, the marriage of his eldest daughter, and the ransoming of
his own body if captured in war, which, fortunately, Henry never was.
He was also able to levy distraint of knighthood, the medieval practice
of forcing those with an annual income of £40 or more to become
knights, in order to form the cavalry to fight for the king in time of

war. Henry fully exploited these rights, even receiving £30,000 in 1504 for the knighting of Prince Arthur 15 years earlier, although he had since died, and for the marriage of the Princess Margaret to the King of Scotland which had taken place in 1502! The act said:

> 1 Forasmuch as the King our Sovereign Lord is rightfully entitled to have two reasonable aids according to the laws of this land, the one aid for the making knight of the right noble Prince his first begotten Prince of Wales deceased, whose soul God pardon, and the other aid for the
> 5 marriage of the right noble Princess his first begotten daughter Margaret, now married unto the King of Scots; and also that his Highness hath sustained and borne great and inestimable charges for the defence of this his realm, and for a firm and a perpetual peace with the realm of Scotland ... the Commons in this present Parliament
> 10 assemblied, considering the premises, and that if the same aids should either of them be levied ... have made humble petition to his Highness graciously to accept and take of them the sum of £40,000 ... And also his Grace ... right well pleased with the said loving offer and grant of his subjects by them so made ... hath pardoned, remitted and released
> 15 the sum of £10,000 ... and is content to accept the sum of £30,000 only in full recompense and satisfaction ...

e) The French Pension

As part of the Treaty of Étaples in 1492 Henry negotiated a pension from the king of France, a similar policy to that followed by Edward IV. In practice, both kings were bribed by their French counterparts to remove their armies from French soil. Henry was promised £159,000 to compensate him for the cost of the war and it was to be paid in annual amounts of about £5,000. This was obviously a useful extra sum at the king's disposal.

f) Bonds and Recognisances

i) Definitions
Henry also exploited another source of raising extraordinary revenue through bonds and recognisances. In general terms this was the practice of subjects paying a sum of money to the crown as a guarantee of their future good behaviour. However, there was a subtle difference between the two. Bonds were written obligations in which people promised to perform some specific action or to pay a sum of money if they failed to carry out their promise. Recognisances were formal acknowledgements of actual debts or other obligations that already existed. Bonds had long been used as a condition for the appointment of officials, particularly customs staff, but in the later fifteenth century their use was extended to private individuals as a way of keeping the peace and ensuring loyalty to the government. Under Henry,

recognisances became the normal way of ensuring payment of legal debts owed to the crown. Such was Henry's personal interest in such matters that none were issued without his explicit agreement. Almost immediately after Bosworth, he demanded £10,000 from Viscount Beaumont of Powicke and a similar sum from the Earl of Westmorland as guarantees of their loyalty in the future. However, most of these commitments entered into with the king were for routine transactions, such as merchants who postponed payment of customs duties. Others were somewhat dubious, even though the original causes were legal enough – for example, recognisances to cover large fines imposed by the courts; but the practice became very questionable when bonds were made for the release of criminals from prison or for the pardon of murderers. At its best, and certainly in those early insecure years of his reign, this financial screw was an effective way of restoring law and order and the evidence shows that in most cases Henry did not even have to collect the sum in full to achieve this from his mightier subjects. Whether or not the practice was morally right is debatable.

ii) Did Henry exploit this Financial Expedient?

In the first decade of the reign 191 bonds were collected, although the policy is usually associated with Henry's later years, when even more bonds were collected. The growth in the activity is well reflected by the fact that the receipts from bonds rose from £3,000 in 1493 to £35,000 in 1505. Those who fell behind in these payments were hounded by the king's officials, particularly with the rise in importance of the Council Learned in the Law (see page 58), which was made responsible for the imposition and assessment of bonds and recognisances. It became greatly feared because of the efficiency of two of its officials, Empson and Dudley, in pursuing defaulters. Indeed, after Dudley's arrival, the records of the council trebled! Professor Lander has noted that out of 62 noble families in existence during Henry's reign, 46 were at one time or another financially at his mercy: 7 were under attainder, 36 were bound by recognisances or obligations, and 3 by other means. It is from such evidence that some historians have concluded that Henry's main aim in using bonds and recognisances was to fill his coffers, and so his reputation for avarice grew, particularly in relation to the later years of the reign. However, the receipts tell us more than this, as in the case of the Earl of Northumberland. Dudley recorded that Henry only intended to make him pay £2,000, although he was originally made to promise much more. This seems to suggest that Henry's chief concern was to threaten financial ruin in order to maintain his subjects' loyalty rather than merely to increase his income.

Henry's reputation for being so rapacious is based on what Polydore Vergil wrote in his *Anglica Historia* having visited England to collect papal taxes:

1 The King wished to keep all Englishmen obedient through fear, and he
considered that whenever they gave him offence they were actuated by
their great wealth ... All of his subjects who were men of substance
when found guilty of whatever fault he harshly fined in order by a
5 penalty which especially deprives of their fortunes not only the men
themselves but even their descendants, to make the population less
well able to undertake any upheaval and to discourage at the same time
all offences.

When describing the later years of the reign Vergil writes that the
people 'considered they were suffering not on account of their own
sins but on account of the greed of their monarch'. There is perhaps
more to this than greed. After the death of Prince Arthur, in 1502, followed shortly afterwards by that of his wife, Henry must have felt that
the security of his dynasty was fast slipping away. This policy of increasingly binding his noble subjects to him financially was an attempt to
avoid this. Nevertheless, it was a policy fraught with danger for in
accumulating this money, both potential and actual, from his nobility, Henry ran the risk of alienating the very people he would need if
his throne were threatened. It was a point noted by a foreign visitor,
the ambassador from Florence, who said that 'The king is very powerful in money, but if fortune allowed some lord of the blood to rise and
he had to take the field, he would fare badly owing to his avarice; his
people would abandon him.'

Historians continue to argue over how rapacious Henry's financial
extortions were. The main conclusions they have reached are that
there was nothing unusual in the collection of Henry's ordinary revenue and that, if anything, it could be described as casual, except over
customs duties. On the other hand, it is clear that with his extraordinary revenue he was energetic in enforcing his feudal prerogatives
and, although technically within the bounds of the law, that he did
stretch them beyond what could be considered a reasonable limit. It
is thought that with bonds and recognisances Henry was guilty of
exploiting the system shamelessly, especially after 1502. Although his
policy can be defended in part by arguing that the full sum due was
rarely collected, receipts show that the amounts received were still
unreasonably high. This view was supported by the confession made
by Edmund Dudley shortly after he was arrested and before his
execution for treason on the accession of Henry VIII. In this statement he cited 84 cases where he believed people had been unjustly
forced to pay. He did not deliberately intend to discredit Henry, but
to make restitution to those 'persons by his grace wronged contrary to
the order of his laws' and so to 'win help and relief for the dead king's
soul'. Indeed, he actually made excuses for his master:

1 It were against reason and good conscience, these matter of bonds
should be reputed as perfect debt: for I think verily his inward mind was
never to use them, of these there are very many. [Here are a few
examples:]

5 Item Sir Nicholas Vaux and Sir Thomas Parr paid 9,000 marks upon a very light ground.
Item the Abbot of Furness had a hard end for his pardon for he paid and is deemed to pay 500 marks for a little matter.
Item a poor gentleman of Kent called Roger Appleton paid 100 marks
10 upon an untrue matter.
Item doctor Horsey was long in prison and paid £100 in my mind contrary to conscience.

These examples and others like them do seem to condemn the king because it seems that Dudley had no reason to lie at this stage. Perhaps Henry provided the final evidence against himself when he made provision in his will for a committee to investigate:

The circumstances if any person of what degree so ever he be, show by any complaint to our executors any wrong to have been done to him, by us, by our commandment, occasion or mean, or that we held any goods or lands which of right ought to appertain to him.

Henry VIII certainly did nothing to stop the exaggerated statements of his father's financial exactions which appeared after his death. This has only added to Henry VII's reputation for rapaciousness.

6 Conclusion: How Rapacious was Henry VII?

> **KEY ISSUE** Was Henry unnecessarily avaricious or just ruthlessly efficient?

The debate about how rapacious Henry was in his financial policy continues. No-one can dispute that he made the most extensive use of many of the means at his disposal to improve his financial position. Compared to those who had gone before and those who were to follow, he appears to have been obsessed with making money. Yet, as the lavishness of his court shows clearly, he was not the miserly king of myth. His 'obsession' may have been due, in part, to the relative poverty and minimal financial experience of his early years in exile. In the words of his modern biographer, S.B. Chrimes, 'No man has ascended the throne with such a lack of financial experience and resources as did Henry.' His methods were certainly stringent, bordering on the tenacious, and naturally became the subject of scrutiny by succeeding generations. As a result, Henry is regarded, both by his contemporaries and by later historians, in a similar way to the new and wealthy industrial classes of the nineteenth century. Then the landed classes sneeringly termed those who had made good through trade the nouveau riche. In the early sixteenth century, as then, it was not deemed proper to take such an active and obvious enjoyment in making money, particularly if you were the king. Yet it was to

England's advantage, in ensuring a continuation of strong and stable government, that he worked so hard and so successfully to improve the monarch's financial independence.

It is difficult to assess accurately the total annual revenue that Henry received because no complete statement was ever drawn up at the time. What we can be certain about is that Bacon's statement that he collected treasure amounting to nearly two million pounds is grossly exaggerated. By the end of the reign Henry's annual revenue was about £113,000, which was a measure of his success in financial affairs. On the other hand, while it is acknowledged that royal financial administration was probably at its most efficient under Henry, recent research suggests that 'the net gain was no more than to restore crown income in real terms to what it had been in the late fourteenth and early fifteenth centuries'. Even the jewels and plate that he left behind him (the contemporary equivalent of money in the bank) was probably worth no more than two years of his gross permanent income. Also it must be remembered that in comparison to its European neighbours the English crown was relatively poor. The King of France, for example, received about £800,000 a year. Nevertheless, Henry had gone further than his Yorkist predecessors. He had not only arrested the decline in royal revenues but restored the solvency of the crown and, by meticulous attention to detail, had inspired a new impetus and greater efficiency into the old financial institutions. Finally, by increasing the annual revenue, his income was nearly twenty times greater than that of his wealthiest noble. Henry had restored to the crown its prestige and given it far greater freedom of action in its policies both at home and abroad.

Summary Diagram
Financial Policy

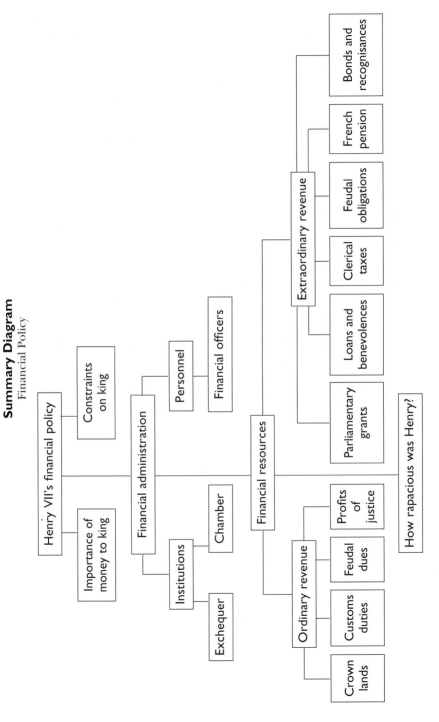

Working on Chapter 4

This chapter is potentially the most difficult to come to terms with because there is a great deal of information for you to remember. The most important thing is that you must make an effort to appreciate and make sense of all the different sources of income available to Henry. You must also try to understand the cause and nature of the continuing historical debate on Henry's financial policies and achievements. The summary diagram should prove an invaluable guide for quick reference. However, you will probably need to test your knowledge and understanding by re-reading the chapter and by answering the following questions.

1. Why did Henry consider that it was so important to improve the crown's financial position?
2. What constraints faced Henry in his financial management?
3. Why did Henry make the Chamber the crown's main financial department?
4. What is meant by ordinary and extraordinary revenue?
5. How successfully did Henry exploit each of the sources of a) ordinary revenue and b) extraordinary revenue?
6. How has history regarded Henry's financial prowess?
7. How rapacious was Henry?

Answering structured and essay questions on Chapter 4

Henry's financial policy continues to be a topic favoured by examiners. It can occur by itself as a structured question or as an essay question that demands an assessment of the reign as a whole.

Study the following structured question:

a) Explain briefly how Henry VII sought to make himself financially secure. *(6 marks)*
b) How successfully did Empson and Dudley contribute to the financial strength of Henry VII? *(9 marks)*

The first question is straightforward and is intended to test candidates' historical knowledge and understanding. Succinctness will be looked for in citing factors such as use of bonds and recognisances; fines; careful accounting; avoidance of warfare and shrewd exploitation of diplomatic negotiations to harvest money rather than expend it.

The second question is rather more difficult in that it seeks to test the skills of historical evaluation and analysis. You should include the following points in your answer:

Both were lawyers, MPs, devoted royal servants and members of the Council Learned in the Law. They specialised in exploiting financial exactions to accumulate finance for the king rather than imprisonment and executions. Their careful accounting and proper financial procedures did much to improve on medieval systems of accounting prevalent in the late fifteenth century. You will need to offer some concrete examples of financial success, the figures for which are easily to be found within the chapter. You may end by concluding that their unpopularity is a measure of their efficiency and success.

Study the following essay questions:

1. How did Henry VII manage to die solvent?
2. 'Henry VII deliberately exploited the rights of the crown in order to make it once again rich and powerful.' Illustrate the truth of this statement and assess the extent to which the king was successful.
3. Discuss the view that 'Henry VII cured the only basic weakness of the English monarchy, its poverty.'

The first question looks straightforward, and in many ways it is. However, it is very easy to fall into the trap of simply writing a narrative describing his financial policy in detail. This will earn you some marks but not as many as an analytical answer will. Now, remembering the way in which we have picked out the key words in essay questions in previous chapters, do the same with this one. This should establish the real core of the question and enable you to analyse rather than describe his policies.

Question 2 involves a quotation. This is a common feature of essay questions at this level. We call them 'challenging statement questions'. Do not be put off by them because they are not as difficult as they may seem. Your first task is to identify the key words in the quotation. When doing this, it often helps to rephrase the statement in your own words. Next, identify what the question requires you to do. You will see that in this case there are two parts to your task – 'illustrate the truth of this statement' and 'assess the extent of Henry's success'. You can tackle this question in several ways: either by considering the two parts separately or by taking each relevant point and relating it to the quotation and assessing its success immediately afterwards. The second way demands rather more planning but is often more effective.

Read the third question carefully. It is another 'challenging statement question', with a quotation that needs to be analysed. You should quickly reach the conclusion that the question is not just concerned with finance. Rephrasing the statement in your own words will help you to spot this. It will also help you to identify the three issues which the examiner wishes you to discuss. What are these?

Source-based questions on Chapter 4

1. *Chamber Receipts, August 1492*
Look at the photograph of the Chamber Receipts with Henry's old and new sign-manuals (page 72). Answer the following questions:

a) It was unusual for a king to sign the accounts himself. Suggest possible reasons why Henry did this. *(2 marks)*

b) In what ways does Henry's signature change? *(2 marks)*

c) Why do you think that Henry altered the way he wrote his initial? *(3 marks)*

d) Look at the last item that he initialled. Why did William Coope pay the king £1,382 4s. 3d? *(3 marks)*

2. *Extraordinary Taxation*
Read the extract from Polydore Vergil's *Anglica Historia* about the benevolence of 1491 (page 78), the extract from the Great *Chronicle of London* (page 79), and the Act for the Feudal Aid, 1504 (page 80). Answer the following questions:

a) Explain briefly:
  i) 'this war' (page 78, line 2) *(2 marks)*
  ii) 'two reasonable aids' (page 80, line 2). *(2 marks)*

b) What was the difference in the way in which the benevolence and the feudal aid were levied by the king? *(2 marks)*

c) Why did Henry only accept £30,000 of the £40,000 offered him by the Commons in 1504? *(4 marks)*

d) How useful are these documents to the historian in gauging the people's reaction to the benevolence and the feudal aid? *(5 marks)*

e) It has been said that Henry successfully exploited his right as king to raise extraordinary taxes in emergencies. How far do these sources and other evidence known to you support this view? *(5 marks)*

3. *Henry's reputation for rapaciousness*
Read the passage from Polydore Vergil's *Anglica Historia* (page 82), the extract from Edmund Dudley's confession (pages 82–3), and the extract from Henry's will (page 83). Answer the following questions:

a) Explain 'The king wished to keep all Englishmen obedient through fear' (page 82, line 1). *(2 marks)*

b) According to Vergil, why did Henry punish all his recalcitrant subjects by financial penalties? *(3 marks)*

c) How does Dudley excuse the king's use of bonds? Does Vergil agree with this view? Explain your answer. *(4 marks)*

d) What do the cases cited by Dudley reveal about Henry's use of bonds? *(3 marks)*

e) Consider all three extracts. Assess their relative importance as evidence of Henry's exploitation of this source of extraordinary taxation. Comment on both reliability and completeness. *(8 marks)*

5 The Economy

POINTS TO CONSIDER

In this chapter you should pay particular attention to three key issues: firstly, Henry's aims with regard to trade; secondly, the extent to which he fulfilled them; and thirdly, their links with wider dynastic matters. In addition, you should note Henry's attitude towards i) enclosure, and assess how serious a problem it was at this time, ii) industry, concentrating on the importance of the cloth trade to the nation's economy, and iii) voyages of exploration, assessing their achievements and what the king hoped to gain from supporting them.

KEY DATES

1485–6   Parliament passed the Navigation Acts which attempted to limit foreign control of English trade.

1489   To protect the crown's interests, parliament passed the first of a series of legislative measures against enclosure.

1496   Trade agreement between England and Burgundy, known as the *Magnus Intercursus*, was signed.

1497   With Henry's support, John Cabot sailed for America which he reached, claiming Newfoundland for England.

1506   Commercial treaty between England and Burgundy, nicknamed the *Malus Intercursus* by Francis Bacon because it was so one-sided in Henry's favour, was signed.

1 Rural Society

> **KEY ISSUE** How and why did the structure of society change?

In the late middle ages the economy of England was largely agricultural, with 90 per cent of the population living off the land. The Black Death of the mid-fourteenth century had reduced the population by about a third. Further outbreaks of plague, high infant mortality, and the ravages of the Hundred Years War and the Wars of the Roses had continued the decline: so the population of England, which had been about six million in 1300, was reduced to about one and a half million by 1450. However, by the 1480s numbers were slowly increasing, although they still fluctuated due to periodic bad harvests and outbreaks of plague.

Historians agree that the events of the late fourteenth and fifteenth centuries fundamentally changed the social structure of

England. In the middle ages society was seen in terms of a pyramid of status, in rank, wealth and occupation. At the top of this hierarchy were the élite groups: the lords temporal and spiritual, knights, esquires and gentlemen. Next were those distinguished by their occupations: the clergy, lawyers, merchants and master craftsmen. Finally came the lowest and the largest group – those with neither wealth nor status: labourers, ordinary soldiers, paupers and vagrants. This pyramidal structure was firmly held together by the feudal system which had been established as far back as the Norman Conquest. Most peasants were serfs who were legally bound to their feudal lords and depended on them for their survival. They had no hope of gaining their freedom. How was this situation beginning to change by the late fifteenth century?

The impact of the Black Death and the subsequent drop in the population led to the relative economic decline of the landowners. Some were forced to lease or sell part of their estates, which created a market in land, making it available to a wider cross-section of society. This led to an expansion in the size of the élites and to them being less exclusive. They became divided into two parts: there were the nobles, whose rank placed them just below the king, and there was the new social category, the gentry, the lesser élite group. The economic crisis also had a profound effect on the peasants at the bottom of the social hierarchy. The decline in the economic power of the landowners began the breakdown of the feudal system. By the beginning of the sixteenth century serfdom was almost non-existent, and the peasants were free to move around the country as they liked. Some took advantage of the availability of land and became commercial farmers. These better-off peasants were known as yeomen. Some retained their small-holdings and supplemented their incomes by working part-time on the commercial farms. Others took advantage of the increased wage levels created by the reduction in the labour force to work for wages. It was this element of choice for the lower orders, created by greater geographical mobility, that was the most significant change in society in the fifteenth century.

2 Enclosure

> **KEY ISSUES** What was enclosure? Why was it once thought to be such a serious problem?

During the middle ages land was farmed by the open-field system in many areas. Surrounding each village there were three open fields which were divided into strips and shared out amongst the villagers. A system of rotation was followed so that the soil did not become exhausted. There was also a stretch of common land where the

villagers grazed their animals. By the late fifteenth century this practice was being challenged in many areas by enclosure. Enclosure was
the fencing-off of land and the abolition of all common rights over it.
It then became solely the responsibility of its individual owner, who
could use it in whatever way he wished, whereas in the open field
system decisions about the way in which the land would be used had
been made collectively by all those who farmed it.

The advantages of enclosure were particularly marked in districts
where the land was more suited to sheep farming than to the growing
of arable crops. The enclosers could divide their land into properly
fenced-off fields, which was not possible with the open field system.
They could then, for instance, practise selective breeding of animals,
or develop their own techniques without being held back by their less
adventurous neighbours. This was particularly true of the midlands
where farmers were still benefiting from changing from arable to pasture farming. The problems resulting from enclosure would also be
most apparent in this area.

Enclosure also brought disadvantages to some sections of the community. It could lead to the eviction of families who could not prove
that they had a legal right to part of the land which was to be
enclosed, or to the loss of the right to use common land for grazing
and for the collection of firewood. John Hales, an enclosure commis-
sioner in the reign of Edward VI, distinguished clearly between fair
and unfair enclosure in this statement to jurors charged with investi-
gating the problem in 1548:

 1 But, first, to declare unto you what is meant by this word, 'enclosures'.
    It is not taken where a man doth enclose and hedge in his own proper
    ground, where no man hath commons. For such enclosure is very ben-
    eficial to the commonwealth ... but it is meant thereby, when any man
 5 hath taken away and enclosed any other men's commons, or hath pulled
    down houses of husbandry, and converted the lands from tillage to
    pasture.

Enclosure was a very contentious issue in the late fifteenth and early
sixteenth centuries and there were many petitions to the king and to
parliament against it. There was also a substantial amount of literary
agitation on the topic. The most famous example of this was in Sir
Thomas More's *Utopia*, published in 1516:

 1 ... Your sheep that were wont to be so meek and tame, and so small
    eaters, now ... be become so great devourers and so wild, that they eat
    up ... the very men themselves. They consume ... whole fields, houses,
    and cities ... Therefore that one covetous and insatiable cormorant
 5 may compass about and enclose many thousand acres of ground
    together within one pale or hedge, the husbandmen be thrust out of
    their own ... they must needs depart away, poor silly wretched souls,
    men, women ... children, widows ... and their whole household small
    in substance and much in number, as husbandry requireth many hands.

10 Away they trudge ... out of their ... houses, finding no place to rest in ... All their household stuff ... they be constrained to sell it for a thing of nought. And when they have wandered abroad till that be spent, what can they do else but steal, and then justly ... be hanged or go a begging. And yet then also they be cast in prison as vagabonds, because
15 they go about and work not ... And this is also the cause why victuals be now in many places dearer.

There were also popular rhymes written against enclosure such as this one in 1496:

The site is bound that should be free
The right is holden from the commonalty
Our commons that at lammas open should be cast
They be closed in and hedged full fast.

('lammas' = a harvest festival when loaves made from the first ripe corn were consecrated.)

However, historians now think that enclosure was not as serious an issue as was once thought. Even in the midlands, where the problem was most concentrated, less than three per cent of the region was enclosed. Firstly, it had been practised for centuries before Henry's reign, so was not a new problem. Secondly, during the fifteenth century, when the population was low and the workforce small, many landlords had turned to pasture farming as the only viable way of using their land, as they could not recruit enough labour to grow arable crops on it. Thirdly, most of the enclosure was done with the consent of both the lord and the tenant. So the much complained of injustices of enclosure must be kept in proportion. In certain cases it did lead to eviction, the depopulation of villages and occasionally vagabondage, but the extent of this has been exaggerated. Unfair enclosure was still quite rare and most of the worst cases of it had already occurred when Henry came to the throne. The engrossing of farms – whereby two or more farms were combined to make a more economic unit – was a practice that was often associated with enclosure and was not infrequently confused with it, even by contemporaries. This undoubtedly had a detrimental effect on rural society, in that it often resulted in people being evicted and made homeless.

Of course, the governments of the time did not have the benefit of historical research at their disposal and they failed to distinguish between the problems caused by enclosure and those that resulted from engrossing. Henry's parliament passed the first legislation against enclosure in 1489, although its terms were motivated by a desire to protect the interests of the crown rather than those of the people adversely affected by the changes. It was specifically aimed at the Isle of Wight on the grounds that the depopulation of the island was a threat to the defence of the realm. Later in the same year another more general act was passed which was the forerunner of legislation in succeeding reigns. Although the word 'enclosure' was not used in the act, its preface did criticise the conversion of arable to pasture, the decay of villages, churches and defences, and unemployment, which it linked to the breakdown of law and order. In an attempt to prevent depopulation, the act forbade the destruction of houses attached to 20 or more acres of land. However, this was never successfully implemented because its enforcement was left to the landlords, who were the very people to benefit from the actions the legislation was designed to prevent. Although it displayed confusion about the practice of enclosure, the act did at least reveal that Henry's government was beginning to accept some responsibility for solving social problems, even if it misunderstood their causes.

3 Industry

> **KEY ISSUES** What was the nature of industry at this time? Why was the cloth industry so important to the nation's economy?

The production of cloth made from wool had become the country's major industry by the fifteenth century, accounting for about 90 per cent of English exports. The manufacture of woollen cloth to some extent healed the wound opened by the change from arable to pasture farming, for which the cloth trade was chiefly responsible. Initially English wool had been exported raw. It was of the highest quality and was consequently in great demand in European markets. English kings were quick to realise the advantages of this and levied heavy duties on its export. By the beginning of Henry's reign the export of raw wool had halved and was being overtaken by that of woollen cloth. Because of the success of the cloth industry it is often overlooked that England was technically backward by continental standards. In the manufacture of commodities such as linen, silk, leather and glass England remained inferior to the rest of Europe. Apart from woollen cloth, England had virtually no manufactured goods to export and the variety of goods imported shows how dependent the country was on industry abroad. As with many industrial jobs at the time, those in the English woollen industry were frequently only part-time occupations shared with agricultural work. For this reason, it is difficult to identify a separate industrial section of society.

The dramatic increase in the export of cloth at the expense of wool made very little difference to England's agriculture, but it did have a significant impact on trade and employment. The expansion of the cloth industry was greatly facilitated by the upward trend in the population, creating a larger pool of available labour. Many of the processes involved in the cloth industry were well suited to the domestic environment and took place in the home: children carded (untangled the fibres) the wool, women spun it and men wove the fabric and sometimes finished it off. It only left the home for fulling (a cleaning process by beating and scouring) and dyeing. The wool was distributed to the outworkers by a clothier who organised and financed the operation. This led to the development of an economic and social hierarchy within the woollen industry. At one end was the family, spinning and weaving and dependent on the clothier for their raw material and livelihood, and at the other was the rich wool merchant, organising all the stages from the distribution of the raw wool to its sale as lengths of cloth in London.

The three main districts in which woollen cloth was manufactured were the West Riding of Yorkshire, East Anglia and the West Country. In some areas, like Wiltshire, families were wholly dependent on the cloth trade for their livelihoods. Small market towns, such as Lavenham in Suffolk and Totnes in Devon, prospered from the proceeds of the trade. Such communities as these farmed on a small scale as well, so there was less fear of unemployment than in areas which were totally dependent on agriculture. However, there was always the danger of war on the continent, a series of bad harvests, or a severe bout of plague disrupting trade. This could result in a drop in demand, less money to spend, and consequently people temporarily out of work. Although some could survive these slumps by turning to work on the land, for the totally urban workers there was no alternative but to resort to begging until trade picked up again. Unemployment was a relatively new phenomenon in the sixteenth century, and the fact that Henry's government did not know how to set about lessening the hardship that it caused is hardly surprising.

The making of woollen cloth continued to dominate the English textile industry until well into the eighteenth century, but there were already the beginnings of the production of a variety of other types of fabric in various parts of the country. In Lancashire there was the beginning of a linen industry making use of local flax; this supplemented its reliance on the import of Irish yarn to maintain its output of coarse woollens on which its people depended. Linen making was also carried out in other parts of the country but on a smaller scale. Hand-knitting, primarily for the production of stockings which were worn by men as well as by women, provided extra income for the poorer peasants in the Lake District and the Cotswolds.

There were other non-agrarian industries in England at this time. Tin and lead mining both satisfied the home market and were profitable exports. The main areas of lead mining were the Pennines, north and central Wales and the Mendips; Devon and particularly Cornwall were famous for their tin mining, and their high-quality products dominated European markets by the sixteenth century. There was the beginning of a brass-making industry based on the mining of copper in Cumberland and zinc ore in the Mendips and metallurgical skills brought from Germany. By the beginning of the sixteenth century such exchange of technological expertise with Europe was not unusual. There is further evidence of it in the introduction of charcoal-fuelled blast furnaces for smelting which led to the production of cast iron in Sussex and Kent, the iron-ore areas. The process of paper-making was brought from Europe and, although the first mill in 1495 was unsuccessful, the industry was established later in the next century. Coal had been mined since the thirteenth century and was exported from the Durham and Northumberland fields in particular. By Henry's reign there is evidence that the output of coal was beginning to accelerate because in areas where timber was scarce it was cheaper to transport coal by water than to bring in wood from other areas. Coal was gradually becoming an important source of fuel for the poor, especially in London.

Despite these innovations, England was still industrially backward by continental standards. Apart from the manufacture of woollen cloth, industry was on a very small scale. For the most part it provided only casual labour for a fraction of the population – work which fluctuated with rises and falls in demand and was at the mercy of the seasons and natural disasters such as flooding. In 1500 England could not be described as an industrial country; her industries (except cloth) employed only small numbers of labourers with an even smaller core of skilled men – hardly the beginnings of a capitalistic society!

4 Trade

> **KEY ISSUE** How and why did Henry encourage English trade?

While building up a fortune for himself, Henry did not neglect the prosperity of his subjects. His 'thrifty mind could not endure to see trade sick' wrote Bacon, and he worked hard to re-establish English commerce which had declined and passed into the hands of foreigners during the upheavals of government in the recent civil wars. The king recognised the importance of flourishing trade to a healthy economy, which in turn would strengthen the Tudors' hold on the throne. If trade was to expand then the necessary ships had to be available to carry goods. The importance which Henry attached to this is evident because it was one of the earliest tasks he tackled.

a) Navigation Acts

When Henry came to the throne England's shipping was inferior to its European counterparts. Most of the country's trade was carried in foreign ships, particularly those of the Hanse, a league of German towns which dominated trade in the Baltic and which jealously guarded its monopoly of trade there. Henry intended to break Hanseatic control of English trade with northern Europe, and that of other foreign merchants too. By the Navigation Act of 1485–6 he attempted to limit the foreign grip on English trade. The act forbade Englishmen to load their goods on foreign ships when English ones were available, and reserved the lucrative trade with Bordeaux exclusively for the English. So from 1486 wines from Gascony were to be imported only in English ships on which at least 50 per cent of each crew was made up of the king's subjects. A further act in 1489 stipulated that English merchants should only import goods in foreign ships if no English ones were available. The subsequent reaction from the Hanse and similar swift retaliation from Spain is evidence that it had the desired effect. This is discussed later in the chapter.

Kings of England no more kept a navy than a regular army, because it would have been just as expensive to maintain. However, in time of war merchant vessels could be transformed into fighting ships, so there was an important link between trade and defence. Henry fully appreciated this fact and encouraged wealthy merchants to build vessels of not less than 80 tons, which could be transformed into effective fighting ships when necessary. Yet Henry VII's reign is not famous for its naval record, unlike Henry VIII's or Elizabeth I's. He did not bequeath his son a significant number of ships as some of his predecessors had done: Henry V left 34 in 1422 and Edward IV left 15 in 1483. However, Henry did at least establish the basis of a proper navy, small though it was. What Henry VII's navy lacked in numbers, it somewhat made up for in quality. His ships were bigger, better equipped and more efficiently administered than those of previous periods. The 600 ton 'Regent', which carried 225 cast-iron guns weighing 250 pounds each, was a force to be reckoned with and the forerunner of more effective warships. The king also constructed the navy's first fortified naval base at Portsmouth. Henry was now more than prepared to defend his island kingdom at sea, and had laid the foundations of naval defence on which his son and granddaughter were so successfully to build.

b) The Cloth Trade

Early in Henry's reign, in 1489, an act was passed which forbade foreign buyers to purchase wool until English merchants had bought all they wanted. This was a deliberate move to show the new king's recognition of this flourishing industry. The same act also made it illegal for foreigners to buy wool for manufacture into cloth outside England. This was intended to restrict the export of raw wool to English merchants and by the end of Henry's reign about 30 per cent less raw wool was exported than had been exported in 1485. This was also partly due to heavy taxes on the export of raw wool and the increasing demands of the native cloth industry. Meanwhile the export of woollen cloth flourished and 60 per cent more cloth was being exported in 1509 than had been exported at the beginning of the reign.

Antwerp was the major recipient of English cloth. However, the activities of the pretenders and the changing nature of foreign policy meant that Henry was sometimes forced to find other markets. This was not particularly difficult as English cloth was in considerable demand and buyers would go wherever it was sold. In 1493, when Perkin Warbeck was enjoying the support of Margaret of Burgundy, Henry issued an embargo against trade with the Netherlands and ordered the Merchant Adventurers, who exported most English cloth, to move to Calais. The ruler of the Netherlands responded with a counter-embargo on English trade. This situation benefited no-one and so, with the failure of Warbeck and the need of Philip of Burgundy to acquire English support against France, the *Magnus Intercursus* was signed in 1496. This treaty stated that English merchants would be allowed to sell their goods wholesale anywhere in the Duke of Burgundy's dominions, except Flanders, without paying any tolls or customs. They would also receive impartial justice in the local courts. This could have provided a foundation upon which healthy commercial relations could be built as it was fair to both sides, but the Merchant Adventurers continued to come into frequent conflict with the government of the Netherlands. There were continued disputes as Philip first tried unsuccessfully to impose a new import duty on English traders, and then to confine them to Antwerp. Nor did Henry ease the situation by attempting to negotiate the surrender of the Earl of Suffolk.

Then in 1506 fate seemed to play into Henry's hands when Philip, on route to Spain, was forced by fierce storms to seek refuge in an English port. Polydore Vergil describes Philip's unexpected arrival in England:

1   Henry, having learnt of Philip's arrival, was filled with the greatest joy, realising that he had been given by divine providence the opportunity of laying his hands on Edmund de la Pole, Earl of Suffolk, whom he knew to be in Philip's power ... Philip was followed not long after by
5   his wife Joanna, eager to see her sister Catherine, the betrothed of Henry, Prince of Wales. Here at Windsor, after holding a lengthy conference on a variety of topics, the question of renewing the treaty was discussed. Above all, Henry sought that the Earl Edmund should be handed over to him ... When Henry promised Philip to spare
10 Edmund's life, he at length voluntarily promised to meet all Henry's demands.

This is a report by Quirini, a Venetian agent accompanying Philip, written at the time:

1 I have exerted myself vastly to learn some of the particulars concerning
Archduke Philip's conference with the King of England and am assured
by several persons that the result is a confirmation between them of
the peace and confederation, with the identical terms and clauses which
5 the Emperor swore three years ago in his own name and that of his son
when at Antwerp, purporting that each of the parties was bound not to
harbour the enemies of the other; and further pledged themselves, in
the event of getting possession of such enemies, immediately to surrender them, especial mention being made of the Duke of Suffolk, called
10 'White Rose', who by this time is supposed to have been surrendered
to the King of England, but on condition that he is to be pardoned and
restored to his possessions.

As Henry's guest, Philip was persuaded to agree to a new trading
agreement. Bacon nicknamed this the *Malus Intercursus* because it was
so one-sided, as these extracts indicate:

3. Trade between England and the Low Countries to be free.
4. English merchants are to be allowed to anchor and remain at anchor in
   Philip's harbours and to trans-ship their goods without any charge
   unless they sell or land them.
5. Philip's subjects, however, are to pay the customary English duties as
   defined by the treaty of 1496.
6. Philip and his heirs are not to exclude English cloth from their dominions nor prohibit their use nor impose any duties upon their sale.

In fact, the treaty was never a realistic basis on which satisfactory commercial relations could be carried out. It was too biased towards the
English. Perhaps fortuitously, Philip died soon afterwards, so it was
never put into practice. Vergil continues:

1 His death was foreshadowed by the unmistakeable portents. That fearful storm which tossed him about for so long and flung him into England
meant nothing else. For indeed in London on the same night in which
he was forced ashore, it happened that the savage force of the gale tore
5 from the summit of St Paul's steeple the brazen eagle ... Now since
Philip was the son of Maximilian, emperor elect of the Romans, who
carried an eagle in his coat of arms, all were convinced by this portent
that the eagle [Maximilian] would shortly suffer a grievous disaster.

In 1507 the *Magnus Intercursus* once more became the basis on
which trading was practised between England and Burgundy. Henry
had used trade as a negotiating weapon to protect his crown: his
policy towards trade with the Netherlands had shown that the security of his throne was his top priority. He had encouraged and stimulated the cloth trade across the Channel and negotiated the basis of
good commercial relations for the future, but he had been prepared
to abandon this at any time that it appeared to run contrary to his
dynastic interests.

5 The Expansion of Overseas Trade

> **KEY ISSUES** What was the nature of Henry's commercial policy?
> How successful was it?

Henry realised that the expansion of overseas trade would boost England's economy and wealth. He also realised how easily trade and dynastic issues could become interwoven and influence the decisions he made. However, it is difficult to identify any consistency in his commercial policy. It was primarily opportunist, and the desire to secure trading advantages always took second place to the need to guarantee the peace and security of the realm.

Henry was keen to extend English trade abroad, particularly as the activities of the pretenders had shown how vulnerable was his dependence on Antwerp. So, in 1486, Henry began negotiating a new commercial agreement which removed the restrictions on Franco-English trade. However, the dispute over Brittany jeopardised this and resulted in higher duties being charged on English goods imported into France. These were modified under the Treaty of Étaples in 1492, but it was not until 1497 that good relations were finally restored by the removal of these impositions. For the rest of Henry's reign English merchants enjoyed unrestricted trade with the French.

Henry was also keen to develop English trade in the Mediterranean, particularly with Florence. This was to counter the powerful influence of the Venetians, who controlled the trade in luxury goods from the east and with whom England had a long-standing tariff war over wines from the Levant. English merchants wished to take an active part in Mediterranean trade and had been prevented from doing so in the past by the Venetians. Their galleys carried most of the luxury goods and wines to northern Europe, and this trading domination was reflected in their high prices. Henry was determined to challenge this. After he had encouraged a few English ships to sail to the Levant and to return with cargoes of malmsey (a strong, sweet wine) in 1488, the Venetians imposed a huge duty against the English. Henry retaliated with a duty on Venetian-borne malmsey and then approached Venice's arch-rival, Florence. A treaty was signed with Florence in 1490. It provided for the establishment of an English staple, the only Italian outlet for English wool, at Pisa, the port of Florence, and restricted England's wool sales to Venice. The Venetians gave in, fearing that their wool supply would fall entirely into the hands of Florence, and they waived the duty on English shipping in the Levant. Henry's aggressive strategy had won the day. Whether the Venetians would have allowed the English to maintain this lucrative position is doubtful but, fortunately for the king, Venice was distracted by the outbreak of the Italian Wars in 1494 and had no time to waste on a petty commercial squabble with England. So

English merchants were able to take advantage of the situation to increase their trade in the Mediterranean.

The most important commercial coup of the reign was a treaty with Spain. The English already had a successful trade link with Spain's neighbour, Portugal, and in 1489 Henry renewed this established treaty. Spain had recently been united to form a single state. Its dominant role in the voyages of exploration to the New World offered exciting possibilities in trade. The Spanish had enjoyed a very favourable position in the reign of Edward IV which gave them exemption from the duties payable by other foreigners (except the Hanse) on the export of English goods. Henry had confirmed these privileges at the beginning of his reign but had restricted them somewhat by the Navigation Acts. The Spanish retaliated, forbidding the export of goods from Spain in foreign ships when native ones were available, but the Treaty of Medina del Campo of 1489 ended this restriction. Although it is best remembered for finalising the marriage between Prince Arthur and Catherine of Aragon, the commercial aspects of the treaty were very important. From 1489 both sides were on equal terms, receiving the same rights in each other's country and with duties fixed at an advantageously low rate. In terms of diplomacy, the treaty was a high point for Henry, but the Spanish never allowed him to become as involved in trade with the New World as he would have liked.

Henry was less successful in his commercial activities in the Baltic. The merchants of the Hanseatic League jealously guarded the virtually exclusive privileges they enjoyed in trade with ports around the Baltic Sea. They also vigorously defended their right, which had been granted to them by Edward IV, to be exempt from duties on goods exported from England, although they failed to observe their promise in return to allow English merchants free access to the Hanse ports. Henry had to tread warily in his dealings over this dispute because the Hanse was well placed to cause trouble by supporting pretenders to the English throne. The Navigation Act was the first blow he aimed at them, but in fact it did little to reduce their privileges. Then he tried to avoid retaliation by confirming the rights bestowed on them in the previous reign. What Henry wanted was to bypass the Hanse and sell English cloth in northern markets where merchants were eager to exchange it for corn and naval stores. The tactic he used was to build up resentment among the Hanse merchants in the hope that they would want to take the matter to a conference. This would give him an opportunity to negotiate the ending of the one-sided treaty agreed under Edward IV. Therefore an act of parliament was passed forbidding any foreigners, including Hansards, from exporting unfinished cloth. A later act stipulated that they were not allowed to take money out of the country. To add further provocation, English merchants who captured Hanse ships went unpunished and German merchants were unable to walk safely in the streets of the capital. The king restricted the Hanse's privilege of importing their goods at preferential rates by interpreting the phrase to mean only goods produced in their own territories. When the conference that Henry had hoped for finally took place at Antwerp in 1491 an amicable solution could not be reached. A settlement only occurred when Henry gave in completely to the Hanse. An act of 1504 restored the Hanse to the favourable position it had enjoyed under Edward IV. This extraordinary u-turn by the king was certainly not dictated by economic considerations. The only satisfactory explanation is that Henry was deeply concerned with the exploits of the Earl of Suffolk who was at this time winning support on the continent, particularly in northern Europe. He must have feared that the Hanse would seek their revenge by supporting this Yorkist rebel. Yet the loss of trading advantage seems out of all proportion to the actual dynastic risks involved.

Henry's other method of dealing with the Hanse was similar to that used against Venice – joining with his target's major rival and attempting to out-manoeuvre them. In 1489 a treaty with Denmark brought English merchants into competition with the Hanse for the trade of Scandinavia and gave the English the right to fish in Icelandic waters. Another opportunity arose in 1499 when a treaty with Riga seemed to create a considerable dent in the Hanse's Baltic monopoly, but this did not last long as Riga soon returned to the Hanseatic League and the treaty was not renewed. So Henry could only temporarily challenge the influence of the Hanse: it was too powerful a body to be overcome permanently.

In assessing the success of Henry's commercial policy it is not possible to reach a simple conclusion. He did undoubtedly increase the outlets for English trade, and he deserves credit for the forward-looking treaty with Spain and the openings he forged with Venice and in Scandinavia. However, his achievements did not, as he had hoped, greatly benefit his financial position. Although the customs revenue rose at the beginning of the reign, this was probably as much a result of the more efficient collection of customs duties as of any expansion of trade. However, English shipping did expand under his patronage and by 1509 English merchants were shipping more cloth abroad than the combined exports of all other merchants. Nevertheless, English trade, apart from that with the Netherlands, was still on a small scale compared with that of Venice or Spain. As in his dealings with the Hanse and the Netherlands, dynastic considerations were always his first priority, and valuable possibilities were sacrificed on more than one occasion in the interests of the security of his regime. Although Henry had opened doors in the Mediterranean and the Baltic, this was as much as he had achieved. What Henry had done was to begin the development of English trade, but it was left to his successors to build on the very limited start he had made.

6 Exploration

KEY ISSUE What was the nature and extent of Henry's contribution to exploration?

One of the most original of Henry's interests was in the geographical discoveries of the age. He gave financial support to John and Sebastian Cabot, as well as to many less well-known men who participated in the exploration of the New World that was being discovered on the far side of the Atlantic. If his successors had followed his example, English domination of the North American mainland might have come about much earlier than it did. However, Henry has been criticised for turning down the patronage of Christopher Columbus at the very beginning of his reign. In fact, the king himself was particularly intrigued by Columbus's proposals to attempt a transatlantic voyage, but the idea was rejected by the council who thought that the plan badly misjudged the size of the ocean. Historians now realise that the decision not to support the venture probably did not rob England of an early lead in the transatlantic race because it is likely that had Columbus set out from this country, rather than from Spain as he did, the winds would only have swept him to the shores of Nova Scotia and not to the more inviting islands of the Caribbean. Henry's obvious regret when he learnt of Columbus's successful voyage to the New World with all the lucrative trade that it offered his patron, Spain, is shown when he seized the opportunity to finance John Cabot.

John Cabot was born in Genoa and was an experienced sailor in the Mediterranean and the east. He arrived in England in 1495 and obtained an audience with the king early the following year. Cabot thought that if he sailed west in a more northerly latitude than Columbus had done, he would shorten the distance to the Far East, which was the goal of all the early westward explorers. Lured by the prospect of the profits to be made from the eastern trade in exotic luxuries and spices, Henry authorised Cabot and his sons to 'sail to all parts, regions and coasts of the eastern, western and northern sea'. However, Henry's cautious nature did not desert him: he gave them £50 for the voyage but would not commit himself to further support until he had proof of the success of this first venture! Unfortunately, stormy weather rendered the voyage a disaster. In 1497 Cabot set out a second time and, after a journey lasting five weeks, land was sighted. Where on the American mainland this was is still uncertain, but the banners of Henry VII and the Pope were duly planted. It was most likely somewhere on the coast of Newfoundland as Cabot comments in his log that there were more cod in the waters than in Iceland. Cabot himself never returned from this expedition.

More successful was the voyage of his son, Sebastian, in 1509. With the blessing of Henry, the younger Cabot sailed with two ships to seek a north-west passage around America to Asia. By now it was accepted that America was a continent distinct from Asia, although, of course, it was not yet known that it was impossible for ships to reach Asia by skirting it to the north. Cabot sailed past the most southerly tip of Greenland and across the Davis Strait, finding an opening on its farthest side. He then found himself in open sea. He was convinced that he had rounded America and was in the ocean leading to Cathay. At this point, because of the dangers of drifting ice, he was forced to turn back by his crew. Nevertheless, Cabot believed that he had found the opening to the east by sailing in a north-westerly direction. In fact the channel he had sailed through was the Hudson Strait, and his new ocean was the Hudson Bay. Sadly, when he reached England with his exciting news, his former royal patron was dead and the new king had interests other than those of exploration. Henry VII has been described as being second only to Ferdinand and Isabella in patronising the discovery of the New World. If the impetus for these discoveries came from Spain, Henry still deserves credit for the encouragement he gave to those brave enough to face the dangers of the North Atlantic. Numerous expeditions ventured forth because of his offer of large rewards to those who developed commercial links with the New World or the east. Due to Henry's patronage, England had more knowledge of North America than any other European country. Unfortunately this advantage was not exploited in the future because of Henry VIII's lack of support for exploration. Mary did renew some interest in this activity but only briefly, and it was really left to Elizabeth to re-establish English interest in maritime activity.

Summary Diagram

The Economy

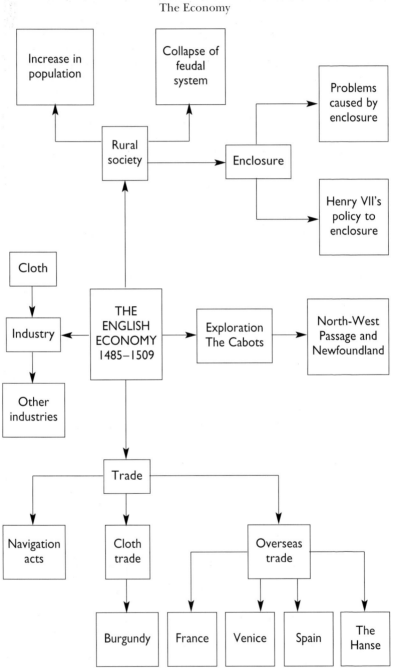

Working on Chapter 5

The most important section in this chapter is the one on trade. Make sure that you understand how and why it was important, especially in terms of the part it played in Henry's domestic (finance) and foreign (diplomacy) policies. You should make quite detailed notes on this as you may be asked to answer an essay question on it. One approach you might adopt would require you to interrogate the information in the chapter by thinking up appropriate questions. The answers to these will help you make sense of the material and enable you to make suitable notes. Below are a list of questions which should prove useful, though you may wish to re-arrange them in an order that makes greater sense to you.

Why did Henry encourage English trade?
How successful was Henry's commercial policy?
How advanced were English exports for the time?
What were the effects of the increase in the export of cloth?
Why were the Navigation Acts of 1485–9 passed, and how far did they benefit English trade?
How did Henry jeopardise trade to protect his throne?
What effect did this have on the economy in general and on the cloth trade in particular?
How and why did Henry protect his trade with France?
How did the king challenge the Venetian monopoly of trade in the Mediterranean?
What did he gain from it?
What commercial advantages did the Treaty of Medina del Campo bring England?
What problems did the Hanseatic League pose in 1485?
How did Henry deal with the Hanse's monopoly of trade in the north?
Why did he suddenly give in to them?

Make certain you include factual information to back up the general points you make. If you answer each question directly it is certain you will have thought through all the important issues the chapter covers, and it is likely you will have gained maximum benefit from the work you have done.

Answering structured and essay questions on Chapter 5

Questions seldom occur on this section alone and you are highly unlikely to be asked structured questions on either trade or the economy. However, in terms of essays, the ideas contained in this chapter are very useful in answering questions which require an overview of the whole reign. The sections on relations with Burgundy and the interwoven dynastic issues can be used in some questions on dynastic or foreign policy. Trade can also be linked with finance. However, questions are occasionally set which concentrate on trade alone.

1. What was the extent of overseas trade in 1485, and what efforts were made during the reign of Henry VII to advance England's commercial interests?

This essay is quite clearly in two parts. The first part is asking you to assess the trade that England was involved in when Henry became king. Beware of spending too long on this section as the core of the question is the second part. It is particularly important when working in the more stressful situation of timed conditions that you learn to work out the balance required in a question and leave adequate time for all sections of it. Now think carefully about the second part of this question. What are the key words? What must you avoid doing? Work out a detailed plan and then structure it to form a suitable and effective argument.

Source-based questions on Chapter 5

1. Enclosure

Read the passages from John Hales' instructions to jurors on page 91, Sir Thomas More's *Utopia* on pages 91–2 and the popular rhyme on page 92. Answer the following questions:

a) Explain the meaning of the following:
  i) 'husbandry' (page 91, line 9) *(1 mark)*
  ii) 'victuals' (page 92, line 15) *(1 mark)*
b) What does Hales define as unfair enclosure? *(2 marks)*
c) Does the popular rhyme agree with this definition? Explain your answer. *(5 marks)*
d) In *Utopia*, what does Sir Thomas More identify as the results of enclosure? *(4 marks)*
e) How accurate a picture of the problems of enclosure in the reign of Henry VII do these three sources provide? *(7 marks)*

2. The Malus Intercursus, 1506

Read the extracts from Polydore Vergil's *Anglica Historia* on page 97, the report by Quirini, the Venetian agent accompanying Philip, on page 98, and the commercial treaty made between Henry and Philip on page 98. Answer the following questions:

a) Explain these references:
  i) 'Catherine' (page 97, line 5) *(2 marks)*
  ii) 'the treaty of 1496' (page 98, clause 5) *(2 marks)*

b) Who was the 'Duke of Suffolk' (page 98, line 9)? Why do both Quirini and Vergil stress his significance in the negotiations between Henry and Philip? *(6 marks)*

c) Compare and contrast the reliability of Quirini's and Vergil's accounts. *(7 marks)*

d) This commercial treaty has been called the *Malus Intercursus*, meaning 'the evil trade agreement'. Using these sources and any other knowledge you have, discuss the appropriateness of this title. *(8 marks)*

6 Foreign Policy

POINTS TO CONSIDER

As you read this chapter keep two questions always in mind: i) What were Henry's aims in his dealings with other powers? ii) How success- ful was he in achieving these aims? In order to minimise potential con- fusion you need to distinguish clearly Henry's dealings with the following foreign states: Burgundy, Brittany, France, Scotland and Spain.

KEY DATES

1489 In order to secure allies against France, Henry signed the treaties of Medina del Campo and Redon with Spain and Brittany respectively.

1492 Treaty of Étaples restored peaceful relations with France.

1495–6 Henry joined the anti-French alliance known as the League of Venice (1495), later renamed the Holy League (1496).

1496 Trade agreement between England and Burgundy, known as *Magnus Intercursus*, ended hostilities between them.

1497 Truce of Ayton restored peaceful relations with Scotland.

1502 Truce of Ayton converted into a full peace treaty.

1506 *Malus Intercursus* forced Burgundy to sign commercial treaty favourable to England.

1508 Henry formed an anti-Spanish alliance known as the League of Cambrai.

▨ Aragonese Empire	1 The Netherlands 6 Saxony
☐ Venetian Dominions	2 Franche-Comté 7 Brandenburg
	3 The Swiss Confederation 8 Savoy
— Boundary of the	4 The Habsburg Lands 9 Milan
Holy Roman Empire	5 Bohemia

1 The European Situation in 1485

KEY ISSUE What was the situation in Europe in 1485?

During the middle ages people preferred to live in peace. They believed this was the way of life that God had ordained for man. As God's temporal representative on earth, the king was expected to maintain this ordered existence. On the other hand, if a ruler was challenged in an aggressive manner by a foreign power, then war was acceptable as a form of defence. In such circumstances kings were expected to win great victories for the honour of their subjects. Obviously, this was a simplistic view of the relations between states and they were far more complex in reality, particularly by the late fifteenth century. Diplomacy in this period had become more subtle and wide-ranging than before. This was because communication was swifter and decisions were being taken by increasingly powerful and ambitious rulers who knew much more than their predecessors of the world outside their immediate localities. This will become clearer as we survey the situation of Europe in 1485, and the factors which influenced Henry VII's foreign policy.

a) Relations between England and France pre-1485

English kings had been gaining and losing territory in France ever since William the Conqueror had first linked England with the Duchy of Normandy in 1066. Consequently, bitter rivalry had existed between the two countries. The latest and most acrimonious contest had been the Hundred Years War (1337–1453) which had resulted in the loss of all English lands in France except Calais. France had finally been able to drive the English out because of the increasing strength of its monarchy which had ended civil conflict and absorbed all but one of the semi-independent feudatories (territories with feudal lords who owed nominal allegiance to the king of France), such as Burgundy and Normandy, into a large and prosperous kingdom. Only Brittany remained, but not for long. Consequently, by the late fifteenth century, France's resources in terms of manpower and revenue were about three times those of its neighbour across the Channel. England could no longer exploit France's weaknesses, nor compete with this enlarged kingdom on equal terms. England's continental ambitions would have to be reassessed by Henry VII.

b) Effects on England of the Unification of Spain

Another factor which would play an important part in influencing the way in which Henry pursued his diplomacy was the unification of Castile and Aragon in 1479, and the consequent arrival of a new power, Spain, on to the European stage. In 1494, when the rulers of France and Spain became embroiled in a tussle for control of northern Italy, the main focus of European rivalry changed. Spain assumed England's traditional position as France's main rival, as the theatre of conflict changed from northern to southern Europe and England was relegated to the status of a second-rate power. English kings had no interest in gaining territory in this part of Europe nor the extra resources available that such direct participation would have required. England's role in the Italian wars was that of an occasional ally, adding extra weight to either Spain or France. However, all too often England was left on the sidelines, and had no share in the rich pickings of victory.

c) Henry's Aims

Henry also found that his position was much more of a defensive one than that of his predecessors. This was because of the nature of his succession, by usurpation. As we have seen, there were several claimants to his throne who successfully sought aid from foreign powers and Henry had to be constantly on his guard against possible invasion. The most vulnerable border was the northern one with Scotland; as Pope Sixtus V remarked, England was 'only half an island'. Scotland was traditionally the back door into England, and one with which the French were particularly familiar.

Polydore Vergil wrote that Henry was 'more inclined to peace than to war'. The situation in Europe, and initially his own vulnerable position in dynastic and financial terms, made non-intervention on the continent the most sensible approach. Henry's foreign policy was very obviously subordinated to his domestic policies of enriching the monarchy and ensuring the obedience of his subjects. Dynastic threats dominated his dealings with foreign rulers.

When reading the following discussion of Henry's foreign policy it will be important to identify Henry's aims and to assess how consistently he pursued them. Following the pattern established by Professor Chrimes, it is customary to divide Henry's foreign policy into three clear phases. The first of these was 1485–92, culminating in the Treaty of Étaples with France; the second continued until 1503, which marked the end of the threat from Scotland; and the third lasted until the king's death in 1509.

2 1485–92: Developing Diplomacy

> **KEY ISSUES** How i) significant and ii) successful were Henry's treaties with Brittany, France and Spain?

a) Consolidating Support

Henry's first actions in foreign affairs were deliberately planned to give him time to consolidate support. He had to ensure he had at least nominal support abroad if he was to secure his throne at home. As France had helped to finance the expedition which had led directly to Bosworth, he seized the opportunity to maintain good relations with England's traditional enemy. He immediately negotiated a one-year truce with France which was subsequently extended to January 1489. Although the Scots had been more favourably disposed towards Henry than Richard at Bosworth, he was aware that the traditional enmity might recur once he was the crowned king. Henry desired peace with his northern neighbour, and in July 1486 he eventually succeeded in persuading James III to agree to a three-year truce. The assassination of James III in 1488 and the accession of the 15-year-old James IV meant that, for a short while at least, Henry had little to fear from across the border. However, he was wise enough to keep his contacts at the Scottish court in case of future aggression.

In spite of the truce with France, in July 1486 Henry negotiated a commercial treaty with Brittany, the other country to offer him hospitality during the long years in exile. Finally, in January 1487 he renewed Edward IV's treaty with Maximilian, king of the Romans, the heir to the Holy Roman Emperor, for one year. So Henry had done his best to ensure that he would not suffer invasion while he was securing his throne at home. For the time being at least he was fairly confident that foreign powers would not offer assistance to the other claimants to the throne. Perhaps most importantly for Henry, these treaties revealed that he was accepted as king of England by his European counterparts and that they expected him to remain so.

b) Problems caused by the Simnel Rising

It was the pretender Lambert Simnel who led Henry to play a more active role in foreign affairs than he had originally intended. Simnel caused various diplomatic problems because he received support from Ireland and Burgundy. The Irish were traditionally opposed to any king of England and were always prepared to support alternative claimants to the English throne. Whereas Irish antagonism was not unusual, that of Burgundy was. Throughout the Hundred Years War against France, Burgundy had been England's main ally. It was also the main outlet for the sale of English cloth. However, Margaret, the Dowager Duchess of Burgundy, the sister of Edward IV, had supported the Yorkists in the recent civil war and was only too willing to provide 2,000 mercenaries for Simnel's cause. Fortunately, other support for Simnel was very limited and Henry was able to defeat the rebels at the Battle of Stoke in 1487. However, the episode acted as a warning to Henry as it showed how vulnerable his kingship was, particularly when claimants had support from outside the country. At least it did not threaten any of the recent truces, but it did emphasise the care with which he would have to monitor the activities of his neighbours.

c) Brittany

The first major foreign problem of the reign centred, perhaps not surprisingly, on France. The French king, Charles VIII, was a minor, and the regent was his sister, Anne of Beaujeau. Until 1487 relations between France and England remained harmonious, but hardly had Henry recovered from the Simnel rising when he was forced to take up an aggressive stance towards France. The situation arose over the future of Brittany. Anne of Beaujeau planned to marry her brother, Charles VIII, to Anne, the daughter and heir of the ageing Duke Francis of Brittany. The French regent was determined to get her way over this because it would be the final stage in her country's long-standing expansionist policy. Brittany was the only part of the historic kingdom of France that still retained its independence. While Duke Francis was alive the Bretons could try to evade this match. In fact, in 1486 the duke arranged for his daughter to marry Maximilian, who had recently been left a widower on the death of his wife, Mary of Burgundy. He then intrigued with the regent's enemies in France, which provoked her to send an army to Brittany in 1488. Maximilian sent a force of 1,500 men to help defend his future father-in-law, and Ferdinand of Aragon, rather begrudgingly, supplied a further 1,000. The duke also asked Henry for help, which put the king in a rather awkward position.

Henry explained this predicament to a papal ambassador. The duke had provided him with hospitality throughout his long years in exile, so he felt he could not allow France to take over Brittany unopposed. Even had this moral obligation not existed, it would be foolish to allow the French to gain complete control of the southern shore of the Channel, and thus pose an increased threat to England's security. On the other hand, France had also given Henry financial assistance in 1485, and he did not want to jeopardise their fragile truce. So he compromised. He sent several hundred volunteers, under his wife's uncle, Lord Scales, to assist Francis whilst attempting to act as a mediator between the two courts. However, as the Bretons refused to listen, he renewed the truce with France and disowned Scales. In July 1488 the Bretons were resoundingly defeated by the French at the Battle of St Aubin du Cormier. The duke finally capitulated and signed the Treaty of Sablé in which he promised that his daughter would not marry without the permission of the French king, thereby acknowledging himself to be the vassal of the king of France. Three weeks later Duke Francis died (of natural causes) and the 12-year-old Anne became Duchess of Brittany. The French immediately claimed custody of her and the annexation of Brittany by France seemed imminent.

Francis Bacon described the king's predicament in his *History of the Reign of King Henry the Seventh* published in 1621:

1 As to the business of Brittaine, the King answered in few words. That the French King and the Duke of Brittaine were the two persons to whom he was most obliged of all men; and that he should think himself very unhappy if things should go so between them, as he should not be
5 able to acquit himself in gratitude towards them both; and that there was no means for him, as a Christian King and a common friend to them ... but to offer himself for a mediator of an accord and peace between them; by which course he doubted not but the king's estate and honour both, would be preserved with more safety and less envy than by a war
10 ... he was utterly unwilling ... to enter into a war with France. A fame of a war he liked well, but not an achievement; for the one he thought would make him richer, and the other poorer; and he was possessed with many secret fears touching his own people, which he was therefore loth to arm, and put weapons into their hands. Yet notwithstand-
15 ing (as a prudent and courageous prince) he was not so averse from a war but that he was resolved to choose it rather than to have Brittaine carried by France; being so great and opulent a duchy, and situate so opportunely to annoy England either for coast or trade.

Henry was once again placed in an awkward position. The acquisition of Brittany by France would make England's main rival even more powerful. It would provide valuable bases for an invasion of England, or for the French to attack merchant ships and disrupt English trade. Yet war would severely strain Henry's finances, which he was trying so hard to build up, and would give France an excuse to help the various claimants to the English throne. Again Henry tried to use diplomacy to save the situation by finding enough allies to deter the French from going to war. He renewed the treaty with Maximilian and, more importantly, made a new alliance with Spain in the Treaty of Medina del Campo in 1489 (see pages 115–16). A treaty was also made with Brittany at Redon in February 1489 in which the Bretons promised to pay the cost of the 6,000 men Henry undertook to send to them. Despite this, Henry's policy was still one of restraint, which was illustrated by the small number of men he intended to send to Brittany. He also continued to emphasise that he was only working to defend England's vital interests, and that he had no intention of waging a war of conquest.

The following is an extract from a dispatch of the papal ambassador to Pope Innocent VIII in January 1489 describing Henry's policy towards Brittany:

1 ... His Majesty himself made many loving speeches about your holiness, saying he had nothing more at heart, than when the preparations of Christendom shall be matured, to proceed against the Infidels; he added

that he was not meditating anything against the King of the French, but
5 he is compelled at present to defend the Breton interests, both on
account of the immense benefits conferred on him by the late Duke in
the time of his misfortunes, and likewise for the defence of his own
kingdom; the affairs of Brittany being so bound up with those of
England, the latter are necessarily endangered by the Breton catas-
10 trophe; and that he has sent ambassadors to the King of the French for
peace, which if effected, all will be well; but if not, he has determined to
defend Brittany and the orphan Duchess with all his might.

Henry dispatched the 6,000 men to defend Brittany in April but,
despite an initial success at Dixmunde in June where his force rescued
Maximilian's garrison, he found himself let down by his allies.
Maximilian's support was rather unreliable, depending on his other
commitments in the vast Habsburg empire and, although he married
Anne in December 1490, it was only by proxy which meant that it was
not legally binding. The Spanish sent a force of 2,000 in 1490, but
they were recalled before the year was out for service against the
Moors of Granada. Finally in December 1491 the Bretons accepted
defeat and the Duchess Anne was married to King Charles. Their
marriage spelled the end of the independence of Brittany.

Henry now faced one of the most difficult decisions of his reign.
He had promised to go to war against France to defend Brittany, but
Brittany was now officially part of France. It seemed that Henry had
to choose between attempting to liberate Brittany by conquering
France, as Henry V had tried, or leaving Brittany to her fate while
obtaining the best terms he could for himself. Whichever decision he
took there was a real danger that France would use her increased control of the Channel coast to invade England. However, Henry was
astute enough to find a more favourable alternative. While he was
aware that England was not strong enough to challenge France
successfully without assistance and that his allies had proved their
unreliability, he recognised that to withdraw without some show of
force would appear weak and would lose him credibility at home and
abroad. He concluded that an aggressive move might give him the
best of both worlds. It would enhance his reputation and it might
have enough nuisance-value to persuade the French to buy him off,
just as they had offered Edward IV generous terms to withdraw his
army from French soil in 1475.

d) Treaty of Étaples, 1492

Henry announced his intention to assert his claim to the French
crown and sent commissioners to collect a forced loan when the loss
of Brittany seemed imminent in the summer of 1491. In October he
summoned a parliament which made a formal grant of two subsidies.
Having spent the year preparing for the invasion of France, the
English army, an imposing force of 26,000 men, crossed the Channel

in October 1492 and laid siege to Boulogne. Because Henry had left his departure until late in the campaigning season, it meant that if he did fight it would not be for long. Fortunately, Charles was eager to be rid of his English aggressor because greater glory was to be won in Italy; so nine days after Henry had set foot on French soil Charles offered peace and on 3 November the Treaty of Étaples was concluded. Charles's only concerns were to keep Brittany and to get rid of Henry. Therefore he promised to give no further aid to English rebels, particularly Warbeck, and to pay the arrears of the Treaty of Picquigny and most of Henry's costs of intervening in Brittany. This totalled 745,000 gold crowns, payable at the rate of 50,000 crowns a year. In contemporary English currency this equalled about £5,000, approximately 5 per cent of the king's annual income.

The following is an extract from Francis Bacon's *History of the Reign of King Henry the Seventh*:

1 Meanwhile a peace was concluded by the commissioners, to continue for both the Kings' lives. Where there was no article of importance; being in effect rather a bargain than a treaty. For all things remained as they were, save that there should be paid to the King seven hundred
5 forty five thousand ducats in present, for the charges in that journey; and five and twenty thousand crowns yearly, for his charges sustained in the aid of the Britons [Bretons] ... There was also assigned by the French King unto all the King's principal councillors great pensions, besides rich gifts for the present ... But the truth is, this peace was wel-
10 comed to both Kings. To Charles, for that it assured unto him the possession of Brittaine, and freed the enterprise of Naples. To Henry, for that it filled his coffers; and that he foresaw at that time a storm of inward troubles coming upon him which presently brake forth.

Henry had not won a glorious victory, for the independence of Brittany was gone forever and the whole of the southern side of the Channel, apart from Calais, was now in French hands. However, the outcome had not been completely negative. He had prevented Charles VIII from helping Perkin Warbeck and he had secured a sizable annual pension from the French. Whilst contending with French aggression he had made a valuable alliance with Spain and had also shown that England under a Tudor king could not be completely overlooked in continental affairs. Perhaps it would be unreasonable to expect Henry to have achieved more, given the situation in which he found himself.

e) Treaty of Medina del Campo, 1489

The most significant achievement of Henry VII's foreign policy was the alliance negotiated with Spain in the Treaty of Medina del Campo signed in March 1489. Spain emerged as a major power in the late fifteenth century after the unification of the country in 1479. Initially

England and Spain were commercial rivals, but both were willing to sink their differences in a common animosity towards France.

Early in 1488 Henry suggested a marriage between his eldest son, Prince Arthur, and Ferdinand and Isabella's youngest daughter, Catherine of Aragon, when they reached marriageable age. Catherine, then aged three, was six months older than her intended husband! The negotiations were laborious as both fathers wanted to secure the best possible terms. Finally, Ferdinand agreed to Henry's demands about the size of Catherine's dowry and promised not to help any English rebels.

It was more difficult to reach agreement over relations with France. In the end it was specified that if either country found itself at war with France, the other was to intervene immediately. War was obviously envisaged in the near future, particularly by the Spanish. Their objective was the reconquest from France of the Pyrenean territories of Cerdagne and Rousillon, and in return they promised Henry help in regaining Normandy and Aquitaine. However, this was not realistic, for, although the French might be persuaded to relinquish the Pyrenean territories which lay outside their 'natural frontiers', they were most unlikely ever to contemplate the loss of Normandy or Aquitaine which were regarded as integral parts of the country. It certainly appears that Henry had the worst of the bargain. By 1493 the Catholic kings had achieved their aim in the Pyrenees, whilst doing little to help Henry accomplish his. But Henry himself does not seem to have felt this, or chose to ignore it, and he continued his pro-Spanish policy throughout his reign. Perhaps this was because for Henry his triumph lay in the fact that his dynasty had been recognised as an equal by one of the leading royal families of Europe. This was of major importance to a usurper who was desperately keen to secure international recognition of the legitimacy of his position as king. He celebrated his success by having a new gold sovereign minted on which he was portrayed wearing, not the traditional open crown of England, but the more prestigious imperial crown closed over with hoops.

Here are some extracts from the Treaty of Medina del Campo, 1489:

2. Neither party shall in any way favour the rebels of the other party, nor permit them to be favoured or stay in his dominions.
3. Mutual assistance to be given against all aggressors within three months after the assistance has been requested, the assisted party to pay the expenses, which are fixed by four knights, two from each side.
4. Henry is not permitted to assist Charles, King of France, or any other prince at war with Spain. Ferdinand and Isabella promise the same to Henry.
5. Henry is not to conclude peace, alliance or treaties with France without the sanction of Ferdinand and Isabella, who, on their side, bind themselves to the same effect with respect to Henry.

3 1493–1502: Successful Diplomacy

> **KEY ISSUE** How successful was Henry's diplomacy during this period?

a) England's Role in Europe in 1493

This was Henry's most successful period in diplomatic affairs. Initially this was a result of Charles VIII's successes in Italy. The other European rulers feared that France was becoming too powerful and in 1495 the Pope, Ferdinand, Maximilian, Venice and Milan formed the League of Venice with the aim of driving Charles out of Italy. England was not included because the theatre of conflict was outside the country's usual sphere of interest, but by 1496 Ferdinand had realised that it might be dangerous to exclude England. Perhaps he suspected that Henry wished to preserve good relations with France and was fearful of losing England's goodwill to the French. Certainly Charles appeared to be ingratiating himself with Henry by offering practical assistance against Warbeck. Whatever the reason, in October 1496 Ferdinand and Henry concluded a further agreement for the marriage of Catherine and Arthur. Also in the same year Ferdinand secured England's entry into the revamped League of Venice, now called the Holy League. However, Henry showed that he was no-one's puppet by joining the League only on condition that England was not bound to go to war against France. Ferdinand agreed to this because England's neutrality was preferable to an alliance with France. To Henry's credit he also managed to make a commercial treaty with France whilst maintaining good relations with his allies in the League. So 1496 was a successful year for Henry, particularly as he also concluded the Magnus Intercursus, the basis on which good trading relations were resumed between England and Burgundy (see page 97 for details).

b) Warbeck Rising: How did this affect Relations with other Powers?

The following year, 1497, saw Warbeck finally captured and peace made with Scotland. The full story of Perkin Warbeck has been told in Chapter 2. The significance of his career to Henry in the field of foreign affairs was that he involved other rulers in England's dynastic problem. Warbeck received support at different times from Ireland, France, Burgundy and Scotland. This greatly complicated Henry's foreign policy and at times jeopardised key features of it. This was particularly evident over the treaty with Spain as the Catholic kings did not wish their daughter to marry the heir to an insecure crown. A further example was in 1493 when Henry went as far as disrupting England's cloth trade by placing a temporary embargo on commercial dealings with the Netherlands because Philip and Margaret were offering Warbeck aid. It also highlighted the long-term problem of possible invasion via England's postern gate, Scotland.

c) Truce of Ayton, 1497

Relations between Scotland and England were always tense, with the Scots taking any opportunity to cross the border and cause problems for their overlord, the king of England. The kings of Scotland traditionally owed allegiance to the English kings, although they resented this and were always looking for ways to avoid it. James IV of Scotland was no exception to the rule and, despite a truce made with Henry when he came to the throne in 1488, he took Perkin Warbeck into his favour when he arrived in Scotland in 1495. He even went as far as to give Warbeck his cousin in marriage, which must have appeared extremely threatening to Henry. However, Warbeck's invasion of England with Scottish help came to nothing; he gained no support south of the border and, when the Scots heard that Henry was sending an army to oppose them, they took flight.

For Henry the situation was made worse by the simultaneous outbreak of a rebellion in Cornwall. The people resented having to contribute towards the cost of halting an invasion which was unlikely to affect them. Fortunately, James IV was losing faith in Warbeck and he did not take advantage of this rebellion to launch another attack of his own. Henry was now able to offer terms on which a treaty with Scotland could be based. The truce of Ayton was concluded in 1497, but it was not until Warbeck had been executed that it became a full treaty of peace. This was a great coup for Henry as no such agreement had been reached between the two countries since 1328. The treaty was sealed by the marriage of James to Margaret, Henry's eldest daughter, in August 1503. However, Scotland did not abandon her ancient pact with France. This meant that the peace depended on the continuation of good relations between England and France. But while Henry lived this did not pose a problem.

d) Marriage of Prince Arthur and Catherine of Aragon, 1501

Another of Henry's diplomatic marriage alliances was also achieved in this period. In October 1501 Catherine of Aragon arrived in England with 100,000 crowns of her dowry. On 14 November she and Arthur were married in St Paul's Cathedral. This alliance was now of even greater significance than when it had originally been mooted. Not only did Henry hope that England would play a part in the growing Spanish empire in the New World, but the marriage of Catherine's sister, Joanna, to Philip of Burgundy tied their two countries closer together and provided the possibility of another ally for Henry if he were to need one. The two marriage alliances were the pinnacle of Henry's success in his foreign policy.

4 1503–9: Changing Diplomacy

> **KEY ISSUE** What factors contributed to Henry's decision to change his foreign policy?

a) The Effects of the Deaths of Prince Arthur, Queen Elizabeth and Isabella of Spain on Foreign Policy

This third and final period of Henry's foreign policy was marred by dynastic upsets and changes in Europe that acted against England's interests. The major blow to Henry's policy was the sudden death of Prince Arthur at Ludlow in April 1502, only five months after his wedding. It seemed that Henry's dynastic hopes had been shattered, but within five weeks of Arthur's death Ferdinand and Isabella were instructing their ambassador to conclude a marriage with Prince Henry, the new heir to the throne, and to settle the terms of the dowry. A formal treaty was confirmed in September 1502, but it recognised that a dispensation would be needed from the Pope because Catherine was considered to be related to Henry in the first degree of affinity because of her marriage to Arthur. The required document arrived in 1504 but by then the diplomatic situation had changed.

In February 1503 Henry suffered another personal loss when Queen Elizabeth died shortly after giving birth to a daughter. This provoked new dynastic worries. Two of Henry's three sons were already dead, and with the death of his wife he had no hope of more children to come. As if to emphasise Henry's vulnerable position, Edmund de la Pole chose this time to flee abroad (see page 30). Henry began to consider the possibility of taking a second wife who might be able to bear him more heirs; he seems to have sought the hand of Joanna of Naples, Margaret of Savoy and Joanna of Castile and Burgundy in turn. The once-popular idea that he intended to marry his daughter-in-law, Catherine of Aragon, can be dismissed as it is not based on any firm evidence. His first choice in 1504 seems to have been the young widow, Queen Joanna of Naples, the niece of Ferdinand of Aragon. This match was encouraged from Spain because Ferdinand was keen to strengthen his links with England as his relations with France were worsening. However, this possibility came to nothing because of a third significant death, that of Isabella of Castile, later in 1504.

Queen Isabella's death did not just mean that Henry and Ferdinand were now rivals in the matrimonial stakes, it also threw into question the continued unity of Spain because of the position of Castile. Joanna was her mother's heir to the kingdom, so the unity of Spain could only be preserved if she allowed her father to act as regent on her behalf. However, Joanna's husband, Philip of Burgundy, dazzled by the prospect of a crown to add to his other titles, forced her to take up her inheritance immediately. It therefore appeared to Henry that his major ally might be reduced in status from king of the whole of Spain to that of Aragon. In addition, his two allies, Spain and Burgundy, on whom he depended in case of enmity from France, were now rivals. Henry had to struggle hard to ensure that he lost the support of neither. This explains why in the last few years of his life his foreign policy was subject to sudden changes of direction in a way that it had never been before.

ELIZABETH OF YORK

-Profile-

Sixteenth-century portrait of Elizabeth of York by an unknown artist and based on an earlier original portrait.

Born to King Edward IV and Elizabeth Woodville on 11 February 1465 at Westminster.

Promised in marriage in 1570 to George Neville, Duke of Bedford. Marriage cancelled when Neville's father turned against Edward IV.

Planned marriage to Louis, the French Dauphin, in 1475 came to nothing.

Elizabeth promised by her mother to the exiled Earl of Richmond, Henry Tudor, who swore on oath in the cathedral of Rennes in December 1483 to marry her when he became king.

Married Henry VII on 18 January 1486. The marriage united the Houses of York and Lancaster.

Gave birth to a son and heir, Arthur, on 19 September 1486.
Crowned Queen of England on 25 November 1487.
Gave birth to a daughter, Margaret, on 29 November 1489.
Gave birth to a second son, Henry, 28 June 1491.
Gave birth to a daughter, Mary, in March 1496.
Gave birth to a third son, Edmund, on 22 February 1499.
Elizabeth died in childbirth on 11 February 1503.

1 She seems to have been beautiful, gentle, kind, generous to her relations, her servants and benefactors. Her income never covered her expenses. She was fond of dancing, of music, dicing, hunting, she kept greyhounds, and she may have been fond of
5 archery — at any rate she bought arrows and broadheads (blunt arrows used in hunting). It is well known that Henry VII personally signed the account book of the Treasurer of his Chamber; but it

is less well known that Elizabeth signed her own accounts too. She is still commemorated as the model for the queen on our playing cards.

> C.R.N. Routh, *Who's Who in Tudor England* (2nd. edn., London, 1990)

1 The King thanked her of her good comfort. After that she separated and came to her own chamber, natutal and motherly remembrance of that great loss smote her so sorrowful to the heart that those about her were faine to send for the King to comfort her.
5 Then his Grace of true gentle and faithful love, in good haste came and relieved her, and showed [how by] her own wise counsel she had given him before, and he for his part would thank God for his son, and would she should do in like wise.

> John Leland describing how Henry VII and his wife Queen Elizabeth comforted each other on the news of the death of their son Prince Arthur, from *De Rebus Brittanicis Collectanea* (c. 1530s)

Gold medallion commemorating the marriage of King Henry VII and Elizabeth of York.

b) Relations with Burgundy

In 1505 Henry attempted to establish more amicable relations with Philip in case of a possible break with France. He also wanted to ensure better trading links with Antwerp and to persuade Philip to surrender the Earl of Suffolk. Friendship with Philip at this time automatically made relations with Ferdinand more difficult, particularly after Henry had lent Philip money to finance his expedition to claim the throne of Castile. Henry also considered marrying Margaret of Savoy, the daughter of Maximilian and sister of Philip, which jeopardised the prospective marriage of Prince Henry and Catherine of Aragon. Henry further antagonised Ferdinand by keeping the Princess's dowry, despite her father's requests to complete the marriage settlement or return the bride and her dowry to Spain. The young Prince Henry was even persuaded to register a formal protest that a marriage with the widow of his brother was against his conscience. Henry now began to seek a French or a Burgundian bride for his son. In 1506 Philip was forced to take shelter at the English court because of storms and Henry seized this opportunity to negotiate a treaty with him. This stated that Suffolk should be handed over to the English and that Henry would marry Philip's sister. Finding himself isolated, Ferdinand sought an agreement with France, as Louis XII was glad to see the union between Spain and the Netherlands shattered. This was cemented in October 1505 when Ferdinand married Germaine de Foix, Louis' niece.

c) Restoration of Links with Spain

However, the diplomatic scene was completely altered in September 1506 when Philip of Burgundy died. His wife, Joanna, supposedly went mad with grief and this provided Ferdinand with an excuse to take over Castile. In the Netherlands Margaret of Savoy acted as regent for her nephew, the six-year-old Archduke Charles (the son of Joanna and Philip), although control really lay with her father, Maximilian. Henry's diplomacy had to alter direction rapidly to keep pace with these changes. Fearing that France would seize upon the weakness of the Netherlands to take lands there, Henry tried to restore links with Ferdinand and to strengthen relations with Maximilian. Margaret of Savoy had rejected his proposal of marriage as she wished to remain a widow, so Henry now sought Joanna of Castile as his wife, believing that the rumours of her madness had been circulated by her father merely as a pretext by which to gain control of Castile. It was a desperate bid to maintain the triangular alliance of England, Castile and Burgundy against France. However it was now Ferdinand in the advantageous position; in control of Castile and allied with France, he refused to agree to Joanna's marriage or to send the rest of Catherine's dowry, as Henry now wanted this marriage at least to go ahead.

d) League of Cambrai, 1508

Henry decided that his earlier hope of a triple alliance of England, Castile and Burgundy was unworkable in the existing political climate. Therefore he tried to form a three-way agreement between England, the Netherlands and France. He showed that he was serious about this by revoking the *Malus Intercursus* and reinstating the *Magnus Intercursus* (see page 98). This was intended to placate the Netherlands, although it was clearly contrary to England's trading interests. Then, in December 1507, Maximilian was prevailed upon to agree to a marriage between the young Archduke Charles and Henry's younger daughter, Mary. Henry made a further attempt to win the hand of Margaret of Savoy, but was again unsuccessful. In an attempt to discomfit Ferdinand even more, he offered Prince Henry as husband for Louis XII's niece, Margaret of Angoulême. By 1508 it seemed as though Henry's dream of uniting his Habsburg and French allies against Ferdinand might become a reality. The unifying factor was to be the League of Cambrai, ostensibly planned to finance a crusade against the Turks, but in reality designed to be an anti-Spanish alliance. However, at the eleventh hour Louis XII decided that he dare not jeopardise his understanding with Ferdinand over Italy, and he bribed the Spanish king to join him. So when the League of Cambrai was signed in December 1508 it was as an alliance against Venice, between the Pope, Louis XII, Maximilian, the Archduke Charles and Ferdinand. In the end it was Henry, and not his wily Spanish rival, who was left isolated by this alliance! However, all these rulers continued to express their support for Henry, and the League did not threaten any of England's vital interests. In fact, it had the advantage of turning Europe's attention away from England at a time when Henry VII was nearing the end of his life.

5 Conclusion: How Successful was Henry's Foreign Policy?

> **KEY ISSUE** How successful was Henry's foreign policy?

Polydore Vergil wrote that Henry 'was most fortunate in war, although he was constitutionally more inclined to peace than to war'. The first part of this statement does not seem to fit with what we know of the Breton crisis and subsequent 'war' with France, the only one which he waged. However, the second half rings true. The king did pursue a policy of peace, even if he could not do so consistently because of the fluid nature of Renaissance diplomacy. Henry was cautious by nature but he was also forced by circumstances to pursue a peaceful policy because it was less expensive, and he lacked the resources to defeat his continental neighbours on their own soil. This was why he was prepared to sign the Treaty of Étaples with the French king after he had barely set foot in France. It was not a glamorous policy, but it was probably the only one that had a realistic chance of being successful.

The other factor which constantly influenced the direction of Henry's foreign policy was the need to protect his newly founded dynasty from foreign-supported rebellion. Many of his negotiations with foreign powers, particularly those with Burgundy, were aimed at cutting off support from challengers to his throne and he was generally successful in his attempts. The marriage alliance with Scotland at least temporarily removed one source of potential support for those who wished to challenge his right to be king.

However, it was the Treaty of Medina del Campo signed with Spain which was Henry's major achievement in foreign affairs, even though its gains were temporarily threatened towards the end of his reign. This treaty not only confirmed the recognition of the Tudor dynasty by one of the most powerful European states, thus eliminating yet another potential source of support for rival claimants to his throne, but it also opened up the realistic possibility of an effective anti-French partnership. The fact that Ferdinand's deviousness and unreliability as an ally meant that an Anglo-Spanish 'axis' never properly developed should not detract from the credit Henry deserves for spotting its potential and playing his part in trying to establish it.

It is clear that the main principles which guided Henry's foreign policy were peace whenever possible, because of his concern not to spend money unnecessarily, and the protection of his regime from foreign-backed challenges. However, it should not be imagined that these were carefully conceived approaches from the start. They emerged as the reign progressed, and as it became obvious that they were the most sensible policies to pursue. Nor should it be thought that these were his only concerns, although his desires to advance the cause of English trade and to continue the traditional rivalry with France were almost always kept subservient to his major aims. Equally, it would be unwise to lay too much emphasis on the coherence or consistency of his diplomacy. For example, the deaths of key figures in his own and other royal families in the first years of the sixteenth century meant that he could not pursue an unswerving policy, and they tested his flexibility and resourcefulness to the full. It was to his credit that he was generally found equal to the challenge. In 1509 Henry could be well pleased with the results of his diplomacy. England was on good terms with most of Europe, his dynasty was secure and was recognised by other rulers, and, most importantly, all this had been achieved without draining his treasury of its hard-won resources.

Summary Diagram
Foreign Policy and Diplomacy

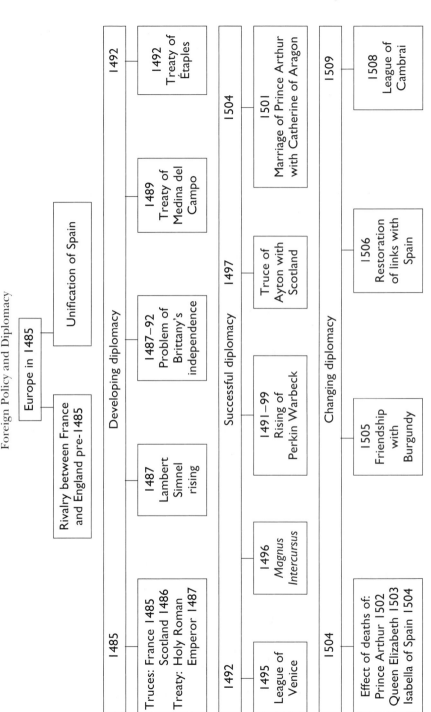

When you make notes on this chapter you must keep in mind two key issues – Henry's aims and the extent to which he was successful in achieving them. You need to be careful not to allow what you write to become so detailed that it becomes impossible to follow the pattern of the argument and to avoid simply making a condensed narrative survey. Your notes should concentrate on recording the general points. The best way of remembering the 'facts' will be to commit to memory the Key Dates of the most important events.

Answering structured and essay questions on Chapter 6

Structured questions on Henry's foreign policy are likely to be specific, focusing on one issue, person or event. The following questions are typical of those asked on this topic:

a) What contribution did trade make to shaping the foreign policy of Henry VII?

b) How successfully did Henry VII counter Margaret of Burgundy's role in encouraging pretenders to his throne?

In (a) the focus is clearly on the issue of trade. In order to answer this question successfully, you will need to ensure that you know a wide range of factual information about the key events covered by this and the previous chapter. It is insufficient just to know what happened, you will need to be able to argue your case clearly and convincingly. The question is telling you that trade did make a contribution towards shaping Henry's foreign policy, therefore, you are left to consider three questions: Where (events e.g. League of Cambrai), When (dates/chronological framework) and How (nature of contribution)? The material gathered here should be sufficient to answer the main question followed by a conclusion assessing the impact trade made to shaping Henry's foreign policy.

In (b) the focus is on the person of Margaret of Burgundy. As always, it is vital that you read the question set very carefully in order to identify exactly what you are being asked to do. In this instance, the measures taken by Henry to counter Margaret of Burgundy are just as important as the actions of Margaret herself. You must begin by clarifying Margaret of Burgundy's role – what did she do, when did she do it, and whom did she encourage. Once you have established this, you can then measure Henry's response and assess its success or failure.

Essay questions on Henry's foreign policy are likely to be synoptic in nature, covering the whole of his reign. Synoptic assessment tests the candidates' understanding of the connections between the different elements of the subject. A typical synoptic question on this topic might be:

1. What were the aims of Henry VII in his foreign policy and how far did he accomplish them?

It is very important in this type of question to ensure that you confine your answer to the specific issues about which you are asked. You must not be tempted to write a narrative account of Henry's foreign policy. A way of avoiding this is to draw up a chart as follows:

Policy	Aim?	Problems?	How successful?
Brittany			
France			
Spain			
Burgundy			
Scotland			

Write a paragraph on each of the events that you have evaluated, remembering to come to an overall conclusion at the end.

Another type of question that can be asked on this topic is:

2. Discuss the view that 'Henry VII's foreign policy was primarily designed to protect his throne and increase his country's wealth'.

The key word here is 'discuss'. Challenging statement questions of this kind require a 'yes/no' answer in which you present the cases both for and against the opinion expressed in the question. Therefore, even if you have strong views on the issue, you must give both sides of the argument. This type of essay is not difficult to plan as long as you consider each side of the argument in turn: events that were designed to safeguard his throne and/or to increase the country's wealth, then those that did not. Such an answer would be made up of an introduction, two arguments (one supporting the view expressed in the question and one opposing it) and a conclusion. You might find it worthwhile to draw up a chart as you did for the previous question. Having drawn up your arguments, you have to decide on the order in which to describe them. Which case would you present first and why?

If you are feeling confident you may wish to attempt a more adventurous approach, and one that normally attracts higher marks from examiners if it is well done. This involves organising your answer as a series of paragraphs, each of which presents the arguments for and against the view expressed in the question on one aspect of Henry's foreign policy. What aspects would you select if you were going to attempt this approach? Chronological periods and countries are two possibilities.

Source-based questions on Chapter 6

1. The Defence of Brittany, 1487–92

Read the extracts about the dilemma facing Henry over Brittany from Francis Bacon's *History of the Reign of King Henry the Seventh* (page 113), and from the papal ambassador's report to Innocent VIII (pages 113–14). Answer the following questions:

a) According to Bacon, what diplomatic problem did Henry face because of the threat of France invading Brittany? *(3 marks)*

b) According to Bacon, how did Henry want to tackle this problem? Was this a typical diplomatic response by the late fifteenth century? *(3 marks)*

c) Compare the king's motives as described by Bacon and by the papal ambassador. *(4 marks)*

d) What arguments are used in both extracts to defend Henry's decision to fight France if mediation failed? *(4 marks)*

e) How far are the sources accurate in reporting Henry's intentions towards France? *(6 marks)*

2. The Treaty of Medina del Campo, 1489, and the Treaty of Étaples, 1492

Read the extract from Francis Bacon's *History of the Reign of King Henry the Seventh* about the Treaty of Étaples (page 115) and the extracts from the Treaty of Medina del Campo (page 116). Answer the following questions:

a) What is meant by 'For all things remained as they were' (page 116, line 3)? *(2 marks)*

b) Read the terms of both treaties. Which was more likely to be honoured, and which was the more advantageous to England? Give reasons for your answers. *(6 marks)*

c) What truth is there in the judgement that the agreement with France was 'rather a bargain than a treaty' (page 115, line 3)? *(4 marks)*

d) How far do you agree with the view that 'the high point of Henry VII's foreign policy was the Treaty of Étaples'? *(8 marks)*

7 Conclusion

POINTS TO CONSIDER

The aim of this chapter is to encourage you to think critically about the question, 'Did Henry VII's reign mark the beginning of a new age in English history?' It draws together themes which have been dealt with separately in each chapter. You should, therefore, have them in mind as you read this chapter.

It was generally agreed from the end of the nineteenth century until quite recently that 1485 marked the beginning of the period called the 'new monarchy' in English history. Historians took Henry VII's reign as the starting point of this period because they identified his rule with the end of the turmoil of the Wars of the Roses and the establishment of a strong, efficient monarchy. They argued that late medieval government had been developing well. They typified it as a system with the monarch at the centre, ruling by consultation with his higher subjects, with a highly developed and respected legal system and with the freedom of the people recognised by the summoning of parliament. They believed that the civil strife of the mid-fifteenth century severely interrupted this progress and that government lost its direction until the accession of Henry VII. The establishment of a new and highly successful dynasty must have seemed the obvious place to start, particularly within the wider context of Europe and with all the dramatic changes brought about by the Renaissance. Historians today challenge this interpretation. They argue that Henry's reign was not so much new and innovative, as essentially medieval in character. Now that more extensive research has been carried out on the government of the Yorkist kings it is easier to see similarities with the government of the first Tudor. Let us review the main features of Henry's reign in the context of the former emphasis on change and the more recent stress on continuity.

Historians who supported the new monarchy theory emphasised the fact that Henry restored the solvency of the crown, rescuing it from the poverty of the civil war. The implication was that he achieved this by employing 'modern' as opposed to 'medieval' approaches. However, it cannot now be maintained that his financial policy was in any sense revolutionary. It is clear that he stretched all the existing sources of revenue to their limit, so that he was not only solvent but had enough savings to make him confident that his son's succession would be assured. But it would be difficult to escape the conclusion that Henry's sources of revenue were not new, and that they were the traditional methods of raising money, familiar to every later medieval king. Where, of course, he was different was in the way he exploited these sources. Through painstaking and meticulous attention to detail he utilised them to the full. For example, his own auditing of the accounts was unique in an English ruler and added greatly to the efficiency of the system.

Another policy of Henry's that was reputedly 'new' was his thrusting of the nobility from their traditional role as advisers of the monarch and replacing them with lesser men. This was not the case. A considerable number of peers served on Henry's council and they were certainly not deliberately overlooked when he needed advice. In fact some, such as the Earl of Oxford and Duke of Bedford, were amongst his closest friends and servants. However, where Henry did differ from tradition was that he did not rely on a handful of favoured magnates. Above all else, he demanded ability and loyalty in his advisers and he promoted men on those criteria alone, rather than giving priority to those with the highest social status. Oxford, Bray, Morton, Empson and Dudley came from a variety of backgrounds; but what they had in common was that they attained high office and remained there because they served their master and their country well.

A further charge made against Henry in his supposedly 'new' treatment of the nobility was the way in which he exploited them financially, particularly in the later years of the reign. Certainly they, more than any other section of society, were forced to pay huge sums of money to the king, but it is important to establish why this was so. It was not, as those historians who support the 'new monarchy' theory would have argued, a further attempt to destroy the power of the peerage. It is true that Henry realised from his own experiences of the Wars of the Roses how dominant the nobility had become during a period of civil war in which the power of the monarch had largely withered away. However, he also understood that its continued existence as a powerful force was vital to the maintenance of social order as he understood it. So his intention was to restore the nobility to its 'proper place' as the leaders of society under the crown. Like Edward IV, he saw that one of the ways in which this could be achieved was by tackling the problems posed by livery and maintenance. However, unlike his predecessor, he allowed no-one to ignore these laws and consequently was much more successful in dealing with the problem. At the same time he also knew that if he was going to be able to use his most powerful subjects to impose law and order in the country at large, he must be able to rely on their loyalty. The system of bonds and recognisances that was used so extensively was primarily intended to achieve this aim. He had no intention of financially crippling any lord who was loyal to the regime.

Earlier historians emphasised the achievement of Henry in restoring law and order after the structure of society had been shattered by the insurrections of the mid-fifteenth century. His achievement in this field was certainly impressive for the period, but it should be remembered that the ways in which he set about settling this problem were very similar to those used by Edward IV – the limiting of livery and maintenance, the development of the role of the JPs in the localities and the establishment of provincial councils. However, there was one major difference. Although Henry's methods were not new, they were pursued more vigorously than ever before. His act against livery and maintenance broke down local power bases built up by ambitious nobles in the past. This, together with his general policy of asserting his rights over the higher nobility, encouraged lesser peers and the major non-noble families to turn to him for support when they were threatened by a social superior. Thus, for the first time, the crown became the arbiter in most disputes between members of the élite groups.

Another feature traditionally identified as part of the new Tudor monarchy was the beginning of government through the household, rather than through the long-established institutions of government. One important piece of evidence that was used to support this argument was Henry's decision quite early in the reign to make the Chamber, rather than the Exchequer, the major financial department of state. But again, later research has shown that there was nothing new in this. Edward IV had successfully used the Chamber for this purpose, and Henry was merely following his example. Early historians were deceived by the fact that at the beginning of his reign Henry's methods of government were naturally traditional as his experience of kingship was so limited. Therefore, initially he used the Exchequer to deal with his revenue and adopted a consultative style of government. He conciliated the peers by consulting them in parliaments and by leading them to war against France. However, the problems of the pretenders, together with increased experience of the shortcomings of the traditional systems, ended this honeymoon period. After surviving the challenge of Perkin Warbeck and the treachery of Sir William Stanley in 1495, Henry seems to have felt utterly betrayed and to have resorted to governing with only the assistance of a handful of trusted servants. Henceforth, Henry mostly shut himself away in his Privy Chamber, where only his most trusted advisers were admitted, and his government became of necessity much more government by the household, because its officials were the only ones who had regular access to the king. This was not the beginning of a steady development in this style of government as used to be thought. Research into the Yorkist period has shown that Henry VII was merely reverting to recent practice. Nor, as is now generally agreed, was this practice continued during the reign of Henry VIII.

So the old argument that the reign of Henry VII began a 'new' age in English history has been discredited by the evidence that so many of the first Tudor's methods were similar to those of his Yorkist predecessors. It has been replaced by the judgement that, although Henry was essentially a medieval monarch, he was an outstanding example of his kind. No other king was so personally involved in matters of state, so efficient in his attention to the details of paper-work or so demanding in the high expectations he had of those who served him.

However, it should not be imagined that Henry had nothing of the 'modern' in him. His reign coincided with the spread of the Renaissance northwards and there is evidence that its spirit had some effect upon him. Certainly, he was prepared to consider exploiting the new ideas and the possibilities for change that Renaissance think-ing encouraged, rather than just being content to do things as they had always been done. He was farsighted enough to foster good relations with the newly-united kingdom of Spain, realising the poten-tial offered by the friendship in any struggle with the might of France. His patronage of the Cabots displayed his understanding of the advantages that exploration outside Europe was already yielding to Portugal and Spain. He was aware of the financial benefits to be gained from any expansion of overseas trade and pursued this as far as his dynastic concerns allowed.

The developments in art and architecture were slow to reach England, but this did not prevent the king from commissioning new buildings. Among these were the Henry VII Chapel in Westminster Abbey, the nave at St. George's Chapel, Windsor, Christchurch Gate at Canterbury, and a new Palace at Richmond. Built in the Gothic style, these and many others were (and most still are) visible reminders of Tudor power, emblazoned with the family emblem, the Tudor rose. Henry used his buildings to display his importance and to remind all his subjects that he was their master. It is perhaps sym-bolic that his tomb, in his Memorial Chapel in Westminster Abbey where he lies with his queen, Elizabeth of York, embodies the two styles of Gothic and Renaissance. The effigies on top of the sarcopha-gus were sculpted by the Italian Pietro Torrigiano in the Florentine fashion, while the bronze screen surrounding them is in the finely detailed Perpendicular style which was unique to England at this time. Like his reign, his tomb was essentially medieval but with hints of a more flamboyant spirit that would flourish after his death.

In April 1509 Henry died suddenly from a stroke. His hard work and determination to succeed had meant that he had achieved more than any of his immediate predecessors. He had brought to an end the dynastic struggles that had for so long rendered the monarchy a pawn of the nobility. He had overcome all potential rivals to his throne, curbed the greater magnates and restored the finances of the crown. Sadly, all this had won him respect rather than popularity. Few mourned his death. Instead, all attention was focused on his son, the new young king. Sir Thomas More spoke for many when he wrote: 'This day is the end of our slavery, the fount of our liberty; the end of sadness, the beginning of joy.' Yet with hindsight, the memorable achievements of the later Tudors were only possible because of the secure foundations laid by Henry VII.

Working on Chapter 7

Studying history at A/AS level is more than simply learning the 'received wisdom' that books and sixth form magazine articles present. It is about learning and using the skills of historical analysis and interpretation and about coming to judgements of your own. It follows, therefore, that you should not be satisfied with taking the analysis presented in this book as being the 'truth'. It is just one point of view. You are expected to read such books critically and from this to be able to form opinions and to present arguments of your own. Of course, in order for you to do this you must first understand the interpretations of the 'experts' before you can begin to challenge them effectively. This is a tall order, and even if you do not feel able to do so now, you may be more confident of doing so when you have completed all your work on the period 1485–1509 or when you are making your final preparations for an exam. To begin this process, you are likely to find it helpful to make brief notes on this chapter, paragraph by paragraph, so as to chart the analysis that is being presented.

Answering structured and essay questions on Chapter 7

It is highly improbable that you will be asked to write a narrative account of Henry VII's reign, but you would be well advised to commit to memory the chronological 'shape' of his reign so that you can select the relevant information for any particular question.

Structured questions on Henry's reign are likely to require you to write about a mixture of what Henry did, why he did it, and what were the effects of his actions. Sometimes you will be asked to give your opinion on a controversial issue where there is no 'right' answer. In such cases it is vital that you supply evidence to back up your point of view.

The following structured question is direct and challenging. The first part is intended to test your knowledge and understanding of a particular feature of Henry's policy. The second part is testing your skills of historical analysis and interpretation and requires you to offer an opinion:

a) Explain how Henry managed to die solvent. *(6 marks)*

You need to know the key features of Henry's financial policy. These include how he raised revenue, how he spent it, and how he saved his money, in part, by following a non-confrontational foreign policy. You should also refer to the expert financial advice he received from shrewd and efficient servants such as Empson, Dudley and Bray.

b) Do you consider Henry VII to have been a successful king? *(9 marks)*

You will find it helpful to make two lists, one under the heading 'success' and one headed 'failure'. When you have decided what factors to put in which category, remember to consider both what is accurate and what some contemporaries mistakenly thought.

General essay questions on Henry's reign are set frequently. Study the following examples:

1. Was Henry VII an innovator?
2. 'He prized efficiency above all things.' Discuss Henry's actions as king in the light of this judgement.
3. How far do you agree with the view that 'Henry's sole innovation was to found a dynasty'?
4. 'Henry VII's achievements, though considerable, were temporary.' What justification is there for this claim?
5. 'Henry VII has been respected by historians for his achievements but, by the time of his death, he was by no means a popular ruler.' Account for the respect and assess the unpopularity referred to in this statement.

First consider which of the questions could be answered by a 'yes in these ways, but no in these other ways' type of essay. However, it might be better to use the two general interpretations presented in this chapter to provide the framework for your answer. You could then conclude with a final paragraph which explains your own point of view.

There are four challenging statement questions. In each case you may find it helpful to rewrite the statement in your own words in order to identify its key words or ideas. The statement in question 2 has two key ideas – that Henry VII valued efficiency, and that this was what he valued most of all. Once you have spotted this, the plan for the essay is very straightforward. You need to show that Henry thought efficiency was important, and then to identify all the other things he valued, placing them in the priority order that you think Henry would have had. You may decide that making his dynasty secure and restoring the monarchy's finances were the activities he valued most.

Each of the statements in questions 3, 4 and 5 also have two key ideas. Identify them. Then think about the exact wording of the rest of each of the questions in order to decide what tasks you are being asked to undertake. In question 5 the key words defining the tasks are 'account for' and 'assess'. What is involved in doing these things?

Further Reading

There are innumerable books available on the Tudor period that cover the reign of Henry VII. However, as the time that you will have available for additional study on the topic will probably be very limited, it will be important that you are consciously selective in your choice of further reading. However try not to limit yourself to general histories only, because they cannot give you the depth of insight provided by well-researched and well-written specialist books.

Of the general histories the following are by far the most useful:
J. Guy, *Tudor England* (OUP, 1988). This is an up-to-date general history and provides a clear view of recent research and interpretations of the reign with useful social and political background on the early sixteenth century.

J.A.F. Thomson, *The Transformation of Medieval England, 1370–1529* (Longman, 1983). There are several relevant chapters on Henry VII in this volume. His reign is discussed in the context of late medieval English history and society, which is a useful perspective for you to acquire.

J.R. Lander, *Government and Community: England 1450–1509* (Edward Arnold, 1980). This provides a detailed and readable account of Henry's reign. Its particular strength is in the way it compares and contrasts Henry's reign with that of his Yorkist predecessors.

Two specialist books written with sixth formers and undergraduate students very much in mind are:
R. Lockyer and A. Thrush, *Henry VII* (3rd edn., Longman Seminar Studies, 1997). A clearly structured and lucidly written text with useful documents at the end.

A. Grant, *Henry VII* (Methuen, 1985). This concentrates on discussing the central themes of the reign. It has the benefit of being both concise and analytical.

S.B. Chrimes, *Henry VII* (Methuen, 1972). This is still the authoritative academic work on Henry VII. It is a very detailed study of Henry's reign and its effect on English history. It would be sensible to read at least a chapter or two in order to acquire some 'feel' of how an experienced and senior research historian dealt with the topic.

R.A. Griffiths and R.S. Thomas, *The making of the Tudor Dynasty* (Alan Sutton, 1985). This provides an outstanding account of Henry's background together with that of his family and of events leading up to 1485.

Some books are especially useful when considering particular aspects of Henry's reign:
B. Thompson (ed.), *The Reign of Henry VII: Proceedings of the 1993 Harlaxton Symposium* (1995). This contains several chapters on various aspects of Henry's reign delivered as lectures by specialist historians.

In terms of its vocabulary and concepts the book may prove difficult to all but the determined, but is worth the effort.
P. Williams, *The Tudor Regime* (Clarendon, 1979). This contains a detailed but clear explanation of the workings and different aspects of Tudor government, and places Henry VII's administration in its historical context.

Henry's foreign and commercial policies are also discussed in books that cover a much wider period. This is useful as Henry's achievements can be seen in perspective:
S. Doran, *England and Europe, 1485–1603* (Longman Seminar Studies, 1986). Written specifically for students, this gives a concise overall view of Henry's foreign policy and includes a selection of relevant documents.
R.B. Wernham, *Before the Armada: The Growth of English Foreign Policy, 1485–1588* (Cape, 1966). This remains the most detailed study of Tudor diplomacy and commercial activities. The text is relatively accessible.

Sources on Henry VII

There is no shortage of accessible published primary material on Henry VII's reign:
I. Arthurson, *Documents of the Reign of Henry VII* (Cambridge Local Examinations Syndicate, 1984). Written for the sixth-form market, this volume contains a wide and varied range of sources, many of which are given in full rather than in excerpt.
G.R. Elton, *The Tudor Constitution* (2nd. edn., CUP, 1982). This is particularly useful for references to documents on constitutional matters.
R. Lockyer and A. Thrush, *Henry VII* (3rd edn., Longman Seminar Studies, 1997). This contains a wide range of documents on different aspects of Henry's reign.
S. Newman, *Yorkists and Tudors, 1485–1603* (Blackwell, 1989). Written with sixth formers in mind, there are several very appropriate documents in this volume. It is well set out under relevant topic headings.
D. Cook, *Documents and Debates, Sixteenth Century England, 1450–1600* (Macmillan, 1980). The first chapter in this contains a selection of documents on Henry and considers how far his reign fits the definition of 'New Monarchy'.
C. Lloyd and S. Thurley, *Henry VIII: Images of a Tudor King* (Phaidon, 1990). Because there are so few surviving portraits of Henry VII what has survived is incorporated in this work on his son. It is both useful and fascinating to read.

Index